A WORKING VACATION IN HEAVEN?

Michael W. Dewar

Copyright © 20224 by Michael W. Dewar

Paperback ISBN: 979-8-9856973-5-3
eBook ISBN: 979-8-9856973-2-2
Published by: Dwelling Place Publishers
PO BOX 360196 · Brooklyn, New York 11236
United States of America
DPSCleansing.com

All rights reserved solely by the author. The author guarantees all contents are original and do not infringe upon the legal rights of any other person or work. No part of this book may be reproduced in any form without the permission of the author.

Unless otherwise indicated, Bible quotations are taken from The Holy Bible, New International Version(NIV). Copyright © 1973, 1978, 1984 by International Bible Society; The Holy Bible, King James Version(KJV), or the New King James Version (NKJV); or, The Holy Bible, English Standard Version (ESV). All Copyright material used by permission.

Dedication

This book is dedicated to all and supporters of this ministry who have stood with me in prayer and other ways over the years. May you receive an extra star in your crown from our Lord Jesus Christ.

CONTENTS

CONTENTS v
PREFACE vii
INTRODUCTION 9
CHAPTER 1 13
A MISUNDERSTOOD EXPECTATION 13
CHAPTER 2 23
WHY ARE BELIEVERS TAKEN TO HEAVEN? 23
CHAPTER 3 39
ASSIGNED TO REIGN ON EARTH WITH CHRIST 39
CHAPTER 4 53
THE ETERNAL REIGN OF THE SON OF GOD 53
CHAPTER 5 65
THE ETERNAL REIGN OF GOD'S PEOPLE 65
CHAPTER 6 75
THE GOD KIND OF LIFE – PART 1 75
CHAPTER 7 89
THE GOD KIND OF LIFE – PART 2 89

REFERENCES……………………………………..…99
OTHER BOOKS BY THIS AUTHOR…………..……….101
ABOUT THE AUTHOR………………………………….107

PREFACE

This book, though standalone, is written as a supplement to my ten-volume series, "Related Events to the Second Coming of the Christ," for this reason frequent reference is made to that series. Some people suggest that I should make this volume eleven of the series. But to me the series is already a complete work; I would rather offer this volume as an incentive to read the entire series, rather than part of it.

So, for those of you who have not read the series, I hope this book will create a thirst for wanting to know more and the series serves as the thirst quencher. And for those who have read the series, I hope it provides a little more to ensure that you are properly registered in the kingdom of God and Christ and ready to reign. The time is short, so review carefully, your relationship with Jesus Christ.

Whether your eschatology (study of the last things) falls into the purview of the series or not, my hope is that no one misses the kingdom of God, because when all is said and done, that is truly what matters. This book makes it absolutely clear what is necessary to meet the qualification to gain entrance into the kingdom of God and to reign with Jesus Christ, eternally, in the world tomorrow. As you read therefore, turn the search light of God's word on in your heart, soul and mind to ensure that you truly know Jesus, and registered in the Lamb's book of Life.

I want to challenge some of you who have read the series, to start a small study group of five or more at your home, office or at church covering all 10 volumes in the series, "Related Events to the Second Coming of the Christ."

Focus on studying one volume at a time, read every scripture reference to get the full flavor and have discussions. This is one way believers can strengthen each other in these last days. Now, come with me through the pages of this volume.

INTRODUCTION

This book is not about the usual discussion about heaven, so from the start let's clear up a few things. First, the Bible teaches that heaven is a real place, and this is true whether you are speaking of the atmospheric heaven, the planetary heaven, or the third heaven where God dwells, or all three. Much is already in print on these issues; they will not be our focus for discussion in this short volume.

Second, this work is not disputing the claim that when the righteous die they go to be with God in heaven, or paradise. The Bible clearly declares that "to be absent from the body is to be present with the Lord" (2 Corinthians 5:1-10). I don't want to take away that hope from anyone, so you can relax and be at peace about such teaching. So, what are we talking about then?

A WORKING VACATION IN HEAVEN?

In this publication, I challenge you to rethink the popular notion that the Lord is returning to take us to heaven, and we will forever live and reign with Him there. Perhaps, this claim makes for happy, emotional preaching, and serve as good consolation at funerals, but it is hardly biblical, the way it is currently understood in places of worship worldwide.

Again, I am not challenging the belief and expectation of the Lord's return. Both Old and New Testament are fraught with the teaching of the coming of the Lord. But you will be hard press to find biblical support for the teaching that the Lord will take us to heaven to live and reign with him forever. The Bible teaches the very opposite to that claim. Yet, it is true that we will go to heaven, and we will reign with the Lord.

But why is it important to get this claim right? Does it have anything to do with our salvation? For sure, it has nothing to do with the provision of our salvation. Salvation is strictly by God's grace alone and it is fully secured in Jesus Christ (John 3:16; Romans 6:23; Ephesians 2:14). If that is the case, why write a book on this small matter?

Well, this is not a small matter at all! It has huge implications as to how we serve and please the Lord now, in this day of grace. God requires faithful service from us, and that is largely connected to the inheritance allotment that will be entrusted to us in the eternal Kingdom of God and Christ (Matthew 25:11-29). What we do now is inherently connected to our eternal inheritance and the responsibility that will be entrusted to us in the world tomorrow, the coming kingdom.

INTRODUCTION

The notion that God gave the life of his Son just to rescue us and take us to heaven is a popular fiction embraced by a wide cross section of the Church. This fictitious belief, perhaps, gave rise to the large number of do-nothing pew-sitters, comprising preachers and church members we have today. Everybody wants to go to heaven, but most of us want to get there on our own terms, not by obeying Jesus Christ!

The disciple-makers in each local church is negligible, most people sit in the wagon dead asleep, while the few do the pulling. So, if you think God saves you just to go to heaven, you are greatly mistaken! This written work prods believers to promptly re-examine that notion in the light of scripture. This examination is critical to the rekindling of the driving evangelistic flames needed to rescue the perishing.

The Great Commission captures the heart-throb and vision of our Lord for the salvation of humankind (Matthew 28:18-20). This mandate was urgently given to the Church, and it is for every member in the pew, not just to the few in the pulpit. The few are supposed to train the many to do the work of the ministry (Ephesians 4:11-14).

We are saved as the workforce for the kingdom of God on earth. We are part of a grand new world order God is building; our faithfulness to Christ now is inherently connected to our future inheritance and leadership responsibility that will be entrusted to us in the coming kingdom (Revelation 21-22).

The teachings of Christ to store up treasures in heaven is connected to His vision of the coming kingdom and our role in that kingdom at the millennial stage and the eternal stage that follows (Matthew 25:31-46; Revelation 20:1-11, 21:1-7).

The rationale of this work is this: "instead of believers going to heaven to reign with Christ in his kingdom—Christ's Kingdom is coming to earth, and we will reign with him on the earth (Matthew 6:9-10). This truth of Scripture holds huge implications as to how we serve Christ here and now. This volume explores these realities to uncovering a treasure trove of miss opportunities as they relate to Christian service and our position in the eternal Kingdom of God and Christ.

God through Jesus Christ and the blessed Holy Spirit is training trusted, faithful, and responsible stewards for the aspect of the kingdom to come. It is for this reason that there will be a *Believers Judgment* to review the quality of our work and reward us (1 Corinthians 3: 8-15; 2 Corinthians 5:10).

The highest reward that will be given are crowns, why? This is what the apostle Paul was looking forward to receiving at the end of his service on earth (2 Timothy 4:6-8). Crowns are symbols of trusted leadership. Jesus wears many of them upon His return to earth because He is coming to reign (Revelation 19:11-16).

We are given crowns because we are returning to reign with him. Crowns are not the only rewards that will be given, but they are the highest. Crowns are given to leaders; leaders are placed over others. Jesus comes back as KING of Kings; that is King over kings, Lord over lords. Come with me, let's unlock some things you should know!

CHAPTER 1

A MISUNDERSTOOD EXPECTATION

Will believers indeed live and reign with Christ in heaven? We will examine the relevant Scripture passages to see if that's the case. The first way some people attempt to answer is to beg the question.

They beg the question by saying, anywhere Jesus is, that is heaven for me. While that response is technically true in terms of personal security and comfort, for most of us it avoids the question. It is not a scholarly answer to an important question that demands a substantive reply; it is inadequate at best, and even disingenuous.

Genuine seekers and critics of the faith would not consider such an answer a reasonable defense of the faith. The apostle Peter instructs us to be ready always to give a reasonable defense to anyone who ask about the hope that is in us (1Peter 3:15). Peter is asserting that the Christian faith is rationally defensible. And he is not alone saying that—the apostle Paul likewise reminds us with these words:

> For though we live in this world, we do not wage war as the world does. The weapons we fight with are not weapons of the world…they have divine power to demolish strongholds…demolish arguments and every pretension that sets itself up against the knowledge of God, and we take captive every thought to make it obedient to Christ. (2 Corinthians 10:3-5).

We do not sit around passively like defenseless sheep, unable to defend what we believe. We demolish strongholds, arguments, falsely constructed and advanced by heretics against the faith. We take captive every thought and bring it into subjection to the authority of Jesus Christ. The Christian soldier stands his grounds and yields no territory to the evil one who is well organized in his fight against God and His Christ (Ephesians 6:10-19).

A MISUNDERSTOOD EXPECTATION

To fight effectively against intellectual and other forms of evil, the believer must put on the full armor of God as the preceding scripture reference prescribes. This includes strong intellectual defense, such as the helmet of salvation and how to wield the sword of the Spirit which is the word of God (v.17). Believers need rigorous study in the Scriptures and other sources to defend the faith (2 Timothy 3:14-16).

We can stand out ground and give strong intellectual and Biblical defense of the faith, such as that given by Rosaria Butterfield in her book, *Five Lies of Our Anti-Christian Age*.[1]

Jesus Invites His Followers to Heaven

During the week of His passion Jesus informed His disciple that He was returning to His Father in heaven, and it was not possible now for them to go with Him; they would follow later. This was not only troubling for the disciples but also confusing. He had been talking about dying and now about returning to the Father. Who is this, Father? they had no idea! How do we get to this place you are going, they asked?

Jesus explained that He is one with the Father, seeing Him was good as seeing the Father. He further explained that He was going ahead to prepare a place and would come back to take them there (John 14:1-14). Believers throughout the centuries have taken comfort from these words of Jesus, and we need not take away anything from what is promised here. Other scripture passages have broadened the scope of our understanding of what is promised concerning heaven. In every case, it is a real place.

A WORKING VACATION IN HEAVEN?

Again, during the week of His passion, Jesus expressed to the Father in His high priestly prayer, the desire to have His followers come to His abode (heaven) to behold His glory (John 17:24). Jesus went back to the Father in heaven forty days after His resurrection (Acts 1:9-11). Every child of God awaits the fulfilment of that promise, and our expectation is not false, but our understanding of it could be misunderstood. We can conclude from these two passages (John 14:1-4 and 17:24) that followers of Jesus Christ are invited to heaven and will go to heaven, because Jesus never reneges on a promise because He who promised is faithful.

When the time is right for us to go to heaven, the Lord Jesus Himself will descend from His abode in the third heaven to the atmospheric heaven with a shout and call for us. He will use the voice of an archangel and a trumpet blast. The people of God, dead and alive will rise to be with Him (1Thessalonians 4:15-18). This phenomenon is referred to as *The Rapture* (Dewar, 2023, Vol.1).[2]

All believers, dead or alive, are awaiting this great exodus from earth to heaven (John 5:28). But as hopeful and promising as that may be—we cannot conclude from these passages or any other, that we are going to heaven to live and reign with Jesus permanently. If you have reached such a conclusion, you may have read your own ideas into the text; you did not get it from the text.

This notion of leaving this world behind to live and reign with Jesus in heaven permanently is nothing short of abandonment of the world. It is a wide-spread misunderstood expectation among Christians. It is a misconception that has motivated some believers throughout the history of the Church to withdraw from the world in ascetic and monastic life. Some have neglected proper stewardship of the earth for this home in another world.

But in as much as we are invited to heaven, the evidence supports a short stay, not a permanent one. It is not the will of God for the people of God to abandon the earth but to shine as light here until the trumpet call to heaven, and even then, there is work here for us to come back to do. So having your mindset on a permanent stay in heaven is a misunderstanding of the promise made.

Many songs have been written with this mistaken notion of abandoning this world to heaven. Yet, Jesus taught us to pray for His kingdom to come, come to earth that God's will might be realized on this earth as in heaven (Matthew 6:9-10). The fact is—heaven is coming to earth. Isaac Watts 'classic poem set to music has it right:

> Jesus shall reign where-ever the sun,
> Does his successive journey run,
> His kingdom spread from shore to shore,
> Till moons shall wax and wane no more.

While other stanzas in Watts' poem are applicable to the Church Age, the first stanza quoted here embraces a broader vision, more applicable to the millennial reign of the Christ over the earth.

The Early Church's Expectation

The apostolic church of the First century A.D. is often referred to as the *Early Church.* The adherents of this movement had the expectation that the ascended Christ would shortly return for them, at most, during the lifetime of the apostles.

This belief concerning the immediate return of Jesus Christ to take His people to heaven, may have partly motivated some believers to sell their lands and give away their earthly belongings (Acts 2:44-45, 4:32-36). But note that I said, partly, because that could not have been the only motivation; most shared their material goods out of love.

The fundamental commands of Jesus were to love God and neighbor (Matthew 5:43-48). So, it is fair to say, the Jesus movement was largely moved by genuine charity to others (John 13:35). But it would be disingenuous to dogmatically assert that was all purely intended. The death of Ananias and Sapphire is clear evidence of other motivations (Acts 5:1-11). The dispute concerning certain widows being neglected in the distribution of food is also supporting evidence (Acts 6:1-7).

It was particularly disconcerting to the Thessalonians saints who observed that the apostles were dying one by one, and their loves ones were also dying, and Jesus did not return. They thought Jesus would return before they die, and now that they have died, what will become of them, are they lost? Others began to say, Jesus came, and they missed the event.

The apostle Paul sought to correct this mistaken belief concerning the return of Jesus Christ in his two epistles to the Thessalonians. He addressed the issue of believers who have fallen asleep or die before the return of our Lord. In First Thessalonians 4:13-18 he says:

> Brothers and sisters, we do not want you to be uninformed about those who sleep in death, so that you do not grieve like the rest of mankind, who have no hope. For we

believe that Jesus died and rose again, and so we believe that God will bring with Jesus those who have fallen asleep in him. According to the Lord's word, we tell you that we who are still alive, who are left until the coming of the Lord, will certainly not precede those who have fallen asleep. For the Lord himself will come down from heaven, with a loud command, with the voice of the archangel and with the trumpet call of God, and the dead in Christ will rise first. After that, we who are still alive...will be caught up in the clouds to meet the Lord in the air. And so we will be with the Lord forever. Therefore encourage one another with these words. (1Thessalonians 4:13-18 NIV)

Jesus did not set a specific date and time for His return to earth. He spoke of His return in terms of what scholars label, "imminent," that is, can happen anytime. Jesus compares His return to the unannounced house break-in of thief in the night. He encouraged His followers to be in a state of preparedness, readiness, and constant watchfulness (Matthew 24:36-51).

The apostles shared that same readiness and watchfulness message with the Thessalonian congregation, warning them that of all people, the Day of the Lord should not take them by surprise (1Thessanolians 5:1-11).

A WORKING VACATION IN HEAVEN?

In Second Thessalonians (2:1-12) the apostle expands the theme of the coming of the Lord, debunking the false claim that the Day of the Lord had already come, and Church folks missed it. This troubling false teaching was widely circulated, causing great concern for the believers.

The apostle Paul shows three events that will take place within the context of the Day of the Lord:1) a great falling-away from the faith (apostacy) will take place first, 2) the removal of the restrainer, that is the Holy Spirit. The Holy Spirit will be called back to heaven, and He will take the Church with Him. The Holy Spirit and the Church are serving now as light and salt, preventing the flood-gate of evil from overrunning the world, and 3) the manifestation of the lawless one, the man of sin, the antichrist will take place.

These three events have not yet happened, and that signals to us that the Day of the Lord did not come, and we missed it as the critics claim. These events are yet to happen. So, there is no need for the believers to be troubled.

The point we are trying to make is that many in the *Early Church* and the centuries that followed, mistakenly believed that Jesus would have returned in their lifetime to take them to heaven. That belief shaped their behavior toward the world. Some withdrew from the world into secluded so-called holy communities or monastic life. Of course, there were other contributing factors such as false philosophies that the human body is evil and needed to be treated with crude severity, thus the practice of asceticism.

A MISUNDERSTOOD EXPECTATION

The attitude then was that this world is evil, and its destruction is imminent, so why practice faithful stewardship toward the earth if we will be gone from here shortly. This attitude, though less prevalent in the 21st Century, is not dead. It has morphed into other negative attitudes toward the earth, even rejection of environmental science such as global warming.

Some Christians fail to understand that they have a creation mandate, a stewardship responsibility to care for the earth. Instead, they are focused on leaving the earth for heaven. But the earth is God's gift to humans; it is our abode, and we need to be good and faithful steward of it.

Watz Disney's world reminds us in a song for children, "It's a small world after all." Louis Armstrong said, "then I said to myself it's a wonderful world." Perhaps Louis is just paraphrasing God's affirmation of "that's good" when He created the earth (Genesis 1:9-31). It's a good world after all. God assigned humans to care for it.

God never gave heaven to humans; He gave the earth. But from the building of the Tower of Babel, unregenerate humans have been trying defiantly to push their way into the heavens. And God allows us the knowledge to explore the outer reach of the heavens, but ever voyage, every trip brings us back to earth. Only those with an invitation will get to the third heaven when God calls for us.

Let me emphasize, we the people of God, have an invitation to visit heaven. The plan of God is to bring the conditions of heaven to earth. We are instructed by our Lord

A WORKING VACATION IN HEAVEN?

to pray for the kingdom to come (Matthew 6:9-10). In fact, it looks like God is relocating to earth (Revelation 21:1-5). So, going to heaven is not a one-way ticket; we who are invited will be coming back to old earth. Perhaps we should keep it clean that the King of the kingdom can say, "Well done!" upon His arrival.

Earth is such a wonderful and magnificent design of unending varieties, and picturesque beauty, yet God is going to do it over, brand new. So, whether old or new, the earth is our domain.

CHAPTER 2

WHY ARE BELIEVERS TAKEN TO HEAVEN?

The people of God will be taken to heaven in the rapture (1Thessalonians 4:16-17). This event will require the resurrection of those "believers" that have died and the physical transformation of those "believers" who are alive (1Corinthians 15:50-54). But why are they going to heaven in the first place? The short answer is—to fulfill a promise Jesus made to them during His first advent (John 14:1-3, 17:24). But that's not the only reason.

The stay in heaven will not be permanent, because believers are seen in heaven celebrating and later returning with Jesus to the earth in what is commonly called, *The Second Coming of the Christ* (see Revelation.19:1-15). For details, see also Dewar, 2023, Vol.5 in the series, "Related Events to the Second Coming of the Christ."[1] There are at least six other reasons believers are taken to heaven during the rapture. The rest of this chapter briefly discussed these.

To Shelter them from Wrath

The Great Tribulation is a period of seven years when the wrath of God will be poured out upon unbelieving humankind and the resources of the earth that make life comfortable for them to live wickedly. This time of wrath will be administered from heaven by Jesus Christ as He breaks the seven-seal scroll of Revelation 6; it is labeled the wrath of the Lamb (Dewar, 2023, *The Great Tribulation Survival Guide…*, Vol.3).[2]

Believers are saved from wrath through the sacrifice of Jesus Christ as the Prophet Isaiah so eloquently stated in chapter 53 of his prophecy. Speaking of Jesus, the prophet said, "Surely he took our pain and borne our suffering, yet we considered him punished by God, stricken by him, and afflicted…he was pierced for our transgression, he was crushed for our iniquities; the punishment that brought us peace was upon him…" (Isaiah 53: 4-5).

Several New Testament (NT) writers made it clear that Jesus, the Lamb of God, bore the wrath of God for His people on the cross (John 1:29, 3:14-18). The apostle John further writes that "Jesus, the Righteous One" is the atoning sacrifice for our sins and the sins of the whole world" (1John 2:2). The King James Version (KJV) uses the term, "propitiation" which means mercy seat or covering.

WHY ARE BELIEVERS TAKEN TO HEAVEN?

The atonement work of Jesus Christ on the cross covers believers from the wrath of God; this is a theme that runs through most of the writings of the apostle Paul. In Romans (1:18-2:16), the apostle describes how "the wrath of God is revealed from heaven against the godlessness and wickedness of people who suppress the truth by their wickedness" (verse18). Paul goes on to explain the universality of sin, showing that both unbelieving Jews and unbelieving Gentiles are without excuse and are under the wrath of God and will face divine judgment according to the light received (2:1-16).

The apostle made it clear that a person is only justified or made righteous before God by faith in the Lord Jesus Christ (Romans 5:1-5). And because they are justified, they stand in grace and will not come under "condemnation" (Romans 8:1 KJV). Again, the Great Tribulation is a time of wrath; the wrath of the Lamb will be poured out upon unbelieving humankind (Revelation.6:1-17).

But just before this time of wrath begins, God will remove His people to a safe place; that safe place is heaven. Jesus descends from the third heaven to the atmospheric heaven, and with the voice of an archangel and a trumpet blast, he calls for the righteous dead and the living, believing, righteous ones. They rise to join him (1Thessalonians 4:16-18). This event is called *The Rapture* (Dewar, 2023, Vol.1).

Immediately after the people of God are removed from earth to heaven, the Great Tribulation will begin. The man of sin, the lawless one, the antichrist will appear on the scene as the global leader (2 Thessalonians.2:1-12; Revelation 13:1-10). His sidekick, the *False Prophet,* will appear shortly after to enforce the antichrist's satanic policies (verses11-18).

The blessed Holy Spirit will be the One removing the people of God from earth to heaven. His assignment began on the Day of Pentecost and will end with the rapture of the Church. He is called back to heaven. Since the Lord himself calls for his people from the atmospheric heaven, Holy Spirit is their rearguard heavenward.

It is not unusual for God to move His people to a safe place before He brings judgment upon the wicked of this world. Before the rain that caused Noah's Flood, God locked Noah and his family into the Ark, ensuring their safety (Genesis 7:11-16). In like manner, before fire and brimstone fell on wicked Sodom and Gomorrah, angels urgently escorted Lot and his family to a safe place (19:15-17, 23-26).

Lot's uncle, Abraham, expected a just God to protect His people and not sweep them away with the wicked. So, he reasoned with God on this question of justice until he was confident God would protect his nephew who was living in Sodom (Genesis18:16-33).

The morning after the destruction of Sodom, Abraham returned to the place of his intersession, where he could see the smoke rising from where the twin cities once stood (Genesis 19: 27-29). Perhaps wondering if he left off praying too early, at ten instead of four or five (Genesis 18:32-33). Lot was safe in the mountains, but Uncle Abe had no immediate way knowing that. The takeaway is—God is faithful to His people, even when they are as flawed as Lot was.

The point we are trying to establish is the fact that the righteous are not taken to from earth to heaven in the rapture for the purpose of reigning with Christ but to be in a safe place until the calamities of the Great Tribulation are over. But that is not the only reason.

To Appear at the Believers' Judgment

Second, believers go heaven in response to a summons to appear before the Judgment Seat of Christ. This judgment is for stewardship accountability and reward (2 Corinthians 5:10). All followers of Jesus Christ are scheduled for this court appearance in heaven. This event is called, *The Believers Judgment and Rewards* (Dewar, 2023, Vol.2).[3]

Believers will be judged for their works, not for their sins. The sin question was settled on the cross; believers are forgiven when Christ is received as Savior and Lord.

We have already established that salvation is a gift of God's grace; it is free. This gift is resident in the person of Jesus Christ alone. You must have Jesus to have salvation (John 3:16; Romans 6:23). We do not earn salvation by good works; otherwise, it would no longer be the gift of God's grace (Ephesians 2:8-10).

Salvation is free but not cheap; it costs God the life of His Son (John 3:16). God saves us from death and hell because He loves us. However, love given should be reciprocated. The way we do that is to serve God in love. Loving service is the biblical way of saying, thanks to God for rescuing us in love. Gratuitous service is done out of love; it is not an attempt to pay God for the salvation received. God's gift of grace does not require payment from us. For that reason, among others, the Lord will reward faithful, loving service.

To Be Rewarded

The believers' rewards are most certainly connected to the Believers' Judgment. This judgment will examine the service we offer to Christ from the time of our conversion to death or to the termination of that service by the rapture. These are the only two events that will end our service to Christ while in the physical body: death or the rapture. The Bible holds much on the rewards and inheritance of the righteous (Daniel 12:13).

The New Testament (NT) is loaded with passages dealing with the believers' reward in heaven, many spoken by Christ Himself in the Gospels. In a few passages, the word "reward" is used interchangeably with the believers' inheritance. But the two are not one and the same: "Reward is earned, whereas inheritance is gifted." For a full discussion on this, see the book, *The Believers Judgment and Rewards* (Dewar, 2023, Vol.2).[4] Again, rewards are given based on the service rendered in the kingdom for Christ in love and faithfulness.

Therefore, if we serve selfishly, we will not receive a reward in heaven for such work. If we serve just for material

WHY ARE BELIEVERS TAKEN TO HEAVEN?

gain, popularity, power, and fame that will be our reward. And those are enjoyed during our earthly life in the physical body.

The Believers Judgment, therefore, is to evaluate our life of service for Christ, to see if it stands up to scrutiny to receive a reward (1Corinthians 3:5-15). In this passage, the apostle Paul addresses the issue of service and rewards with great emphasis on the point that we are all co-laborers in the kingdom of God and Christ and there is no big me or little you. Each is given an assigned task, one plants, the other waters, but it is God who make thinks grow and produce a harvest, not us (1 Corinthians 3:.5-9).

The apostle goes on to say, the day of judgement will evaluate the nature and character of our work of service. Some work will be discarded because they will not stand up to scrutiny. The worker will be saved but his work will be disqualified, and no reward will be received (verses 12-15). A construction metaphor is used here where the builder did not build according to code, and he suffers loss because the inspector rejects the building, and it must be torn down.

In like manner, some believers will suffer loss at *The Believers' Judgment*; their works will be disqualified, and no reward will be received. They will not be thrown out of heaven, because the salvation that gave them entrance to heaven is not based upon good works. It is God's gift of grace (Romans 6:23). In other words, work done in the kingdom and for the kingdom will be paid for in terms of rewards. Rewards are earned based on the quality service offered to Christ; this must be works offered in love and faithfulness.

The people who work for self and not Christ—their rewards are their multi-million-dollar mansions, luxury cars, lavish living, globe-trotting private jets. Jesus said that they have already received their reward here on earth (Matthew 6:1-5,16-18). They have no reward to receive in heaven.

Some will not make it into heaven at all even though they claim to be working for Jesus; they did not receive His gift of salvation. Jesus will say to them, "Depart from me you workers of iniquity, I do not know you" (Matthew 7:21-23). In other words, they have no salvation relationship with Jesus Christ. Good works is no substitute for a saving relationship with Jesus; that is basic to the Christian life (John 3:16).

Sonship Consummation and Declaration

Believers will go to heaven at the rapture for *consummation and declaration* of their sonship. In other words, it is the time that the children of God are formally presented to the Father by the Son, and their identity is declared to the principalities and powers. Believers are made citizens of the kingdom of God by a new birth experience, and they are adopted into the family of God (John 3:5-8; Romans 8: 8-10). Let us now focus on these two words: "consummation" and "declaration."

In the ancient world, adoption was not limited to children, adults were also adopted and given the same rights as the biologically born son (Unger,1988).[5] Adoption was like marriage; it was a legal and social transaction and there was a time laps between the two as between being the pledge of marriage and the consummation of that marriage.

Furthermore, the father was the one who took the lead finding a bride for his son as was the case of Abraham and Isaac. The father sets the terms of the contract. The bride was brought to the father's house after the legal issues were worked out with the bride's father. The betrothal was about a year or more before the consummation of the marriage.

In the case of Mary and Joseph, they pledged to be married, but before they came together, she was found to be pregnant (Matthew 1:18-19). Mary was not yet taken to the father's house and the marriage was not yet consummated, so Joseph sought to divorce her quietly. But God convinced him that Mary was faithful; she was still a virgin. Joseph finalized the marriage but did not consummate the marriage until sometime after Jesus was born (Matthew 1:20-24).

When a marriage is finalized, a declaration is also made to the larger community that these two individuals are husband and wife and some symbol, like a ring, is worn to mark the occasion. When the Prodigal son was received back into the family a ring was placed on his finger by the father to mark the occasion (Luke 15:22 NIV).

The relationship between God and His people in both Old and New Testament is likened to a marriage, particularly a Jewish marriage (Hosea 1-2; Matthew 25:1-13; Ephesians 5:

22-33; Revelation 19:6-9). Jesus by his death and resurrection purchased a people for himself. But He returned to heaven without them. The Holy Spirit was sent to select, seal, and bring them to Jesus for salvation, then to the Father's house.

Jesus returned to heaven to prepare that place for us in the Father's house. As soon as the selection for the Body of Christ is complete and the place Jesus gone to prepare is read, Jesus will come calling for His people; the Holy Spirit will quicken them to rise to meet Him (John 14:1-4; 1Thessalonians 4:16-18). At that time, the children will be formally presented to the Father and be declared to all creation (Romans 8:18-25).

In redemption, we became citizens of God's Kingdom by a new birth experience and adopted into the family of God. By this, we become heirs, and joint-heirs with Jesus Christ (John 3:5-8; Romans 8:14-17). This is a profound mystery.

To Participate in the Crowning of the Christ

Believers go to heaven at the rapture to participate in the coronation of the Christ. The crowning is not covered extensively here, details are already dealt with in my work *Coronation of the Christ...* (Vol.4), series, "Related Events to the Second Coming of the Christ."

In as much as Jesus Christ is always King over the universe, He has never been crowned king by humans. Perhaps that is why He said to Pilate, the Roman governor, "My kingdom is not of this world" (John 18:36). He came to

WHY ARE BELIEVERS TAKEN TO HEAVEN?

establish the rule of God in the hearts of humans. Humans must be first won inwardly, otherwise they must be ruled by force. But God is love and prefers to govern in love.

Satan offered to make Jesus king over this world, but Jesus refused (Matthew 4:8-11). Some of His followers also wanted to make Him king by force, but he rejected them as well (John 6:14-15). His mission was not to be head of government by sitting on a throne to compete with Ceasar, but to provide salvation and to rule from the human heart. But His own people, Israel, rejected Him (John 1:12).

The redemptive mission of Jesus was twofold. First, to provide salvation by the sacrifice of himself on the cross and to rise from the dead for our justification. Second, to call out a people for himself by establishing the Church. The Church is God's embassy on earth, a divine institution.

When the Church completes its mission by bringing all who are ordained to eternal life into the embassy, Jesus will call for His people to join Him in heaven (1Thessalonians 4:16-18). The blessed Holy Spirit dwells in all the people of God; He will quicken their mortal bodies and transport them to heaven. The apostle Paul expresses this truth thus, "And if the Spirit of him who raise Jesus from the dead is living in you, he who raised Christ from the dead will also give life to your mortal bodies because of the Spirit who lives in you" (Romans 8:11; 1Corinthians 15:50-56 NIV).

The people of God will remain in heaven from the rapture to the near end of the Great Tribulation, a period of seven years. During our stay in heaven, we will participate in the coronation of the Christ (Revelation 19:1-10). We will crown him as KING of Kings and LORD of Lords, then we will return to earth with Him to rule (Revelation 19:11-20).

To Put a Government Together

Another reason the people of God are taken to heaven is for the Lord Jesus Christ to put a government together before He returns to earth to reign. He will return as KING of Kings and LORD of Lords. These are leadership titles that will also be given to many of His people. For details see (Vols. 4 & 5) in the series, "Related Events to the Second Coming of the Christ" by this same author.

In the United States, a new presidential administration officially takes the reins of government every four years, on January 20th after the previous Fall general election. The new President does not assume the office alone, he or she comes to Washington D.C. with a government already in place, especially his/her cabinet. In like manner, Jesus does not return to earth to reign alone. He comes from heaven with a government already in place (Revelation 19:11-18). And He returns as the head of government (Isaiah 9:6-7).

The Believers' Judgment and Rewards serve not only as an accountability mechanism, but as screening protocol to determine on whom to confer leadership roles in the new government coming to power on earth. Many leadership titles will be given; kingly crowns and Lords will be among the highest. For this reason, Jesus has many crowns on His head and His title is KING of Kings and LORD of Lords (Revelation 19:12,16). Every believer is a citizen of the kingdom, not all will be Kings and Lords. There are many lesser titles, some are classified.

Again, these titles are symbols of leadership conferred on those who served our Lord faithfully now in the Church Age. Their works of service were not disqualified at the *Believers' Judgment* (2 Timothy 4:6-8; 1Corinthians 3:11-15). From this large pool of faithful leaders, the Lord will choose the key leaders to serve in His administration.

Our faithfulness now in the service of our Lord will impact the position of leadership service entrusted to us when Christ returns to reign. Those who were faithful in little will be entrusted with much, and those who suffered for righteousness' sake now; they will have great rewards in heaven (Matthew 5:11-12). Crowns are the highest symbols of leadership; not everybody will be given crowns.

Scriptural Insights on Chosen Leadership

The Scripture gives us insights as to how we will be chosen to serve in our Lord's government and how our service now relates to the leadership responsibility we will be entrusted. Let's examine three stories, all in Matthew 25: the ten virgins, the talents, and the judgment of nations. All three stories have relevance to the coming of the Lord.

A WORKING VACATION IN HEAVEN?

First, the parable of the Ten Virgins (Matthew 25:1-13). All ten young women were waiting for the coming of the Lord, the bridegroom. Because of their preparedness and watchfulness, half is considered wise. The other half lacked these qualities and is labeled foolish. The wise were rewarded and the foolish suffered lost. The five foolish are not good examples of leadership. They are careless; they lack vision, and they lack oil when it matters most. Oil is symbolic of the Holy Spirit or a genuine salvation experience.

Second, the parable of the talents (Matthew 25:14-30). It depicts three servants who are entrusted with their master's money: one five bags of gold, the other, two bags, and the other, one bag of gold. It is understood that they should invest the money so that the owner will have a profit upon his return.

Two servants invested and doubled their Lord's money and were commended with these words, "well done, good and faithful servant! You have been faithful over a few things; I will put you in charge of many things. Come and share your master's happiness!" (Matthew 25:21-23).

The servant with one bag of gold made no investment with his master's money; he did not even put it in the bank to accrue interest. Instead, he dug a hole in the ground and buried his master's money and was rather insolent when he handed back the bag of gold. He was called a lazy, worthless, wicked, and unprofitable servant. His master had no further use for him in his enterprise; he dismissed him. The story gives us insight about the kingdom of God, God's expectation of us, and how we serve. Our faithfulness to Christ now will impact our reward when the kingdom fully comes to earth.

The third story has to do with the judgment of nations (Matthew 25:31-46). Here the Lord divides people into two groups: sheep on His right hand, goats on His left. He judges them based on how they serve their fellow humans now. One group gave loving, compassionate service to their fellow humans, while the other group was cruel and heartless.

To the compassionate group the Lord says, "Come, you blessed of my Father, inherit the kingdom prepared for you from the foundation of the world: for I was hungry, and you gave me food, I was thirsty, and you gave me drink; I was a stranger, and you took me in. I needed clothes and you clothed me, I was sick, and you looked after me, I was in prison, and you came to see me" (Matthew 25: 34-36). The other group lacks these qualities of compassionate service and is rejected; they are not allowed to reign with Him (verses 41-46).

What is the takeaway from these three stories? If we selfishly, serving ourselves rather than serving our Lord faithfully, and serving people in love, that will negatively affect the leadership responsibility entrusted to us in the coming government of Jesus Christ over the earth. Believers' works will be tested at the Believers' Judgment, and some will suffer loss (2 Corinthians 5:10). Perhaps, this is why Jesus would not commit to any disciple's request to sit at his right or lefthand in His kingdom before they were tested (Matthew 20:20-23; Mark 10:35-40). For these reasons, among others,

A WORKING VACATION IN HEAVEN?

we are encouraged to serve the Lord faithfully because it has lasting implications for our status in the world tomorrow.

Summary

We set out to establish that the people of God will go heaven at the rapture, but not to permanently live and reign with Christ as commonly believed by Christians around the world. Our understanding of living and reigning with Christ is somewhat misunderstood. The misunderstanding, however, is not anything to lose sleep over, it will not change what God has planned for His people.

The people of God will stay in heaven for a short time, at most seven years. And we will be there for specific reasons. Six of which are covered in this chapter. We will return to earth with Christ to end the seven years of Great Tribulation, and reign with Him over the earth for a thousand years; this is called, the Millennium.

Yet, we do not want to abandon the idea of heaven but adjust our understanding to meet what the Bible teaches about heaven and our relationship with it. The heaven we now have in mind is greatly fictionized to the heaven that will be. This issue will also be discussed later. The invitation to come to heaven to behold Lord's glory is not a do-nothing vacation. It will be a working vacation, loaded with activities. People tend to have a fictitious view of heaven such as glorified humans, dressed in long white robes loafing around all day.

CHAPTER 3

ASSIGNED TO REIGN ON EARTH WITH CHRIST

The Christian mindset of going to heaven at the end of their earthly life to live and reign with Christ is not heretical, but widely misunderstood. And it has positive and negative implications. On the one hand, it causes some believers to be so heavenly minded, they are no earthly good. While on the other hand, some are so materialistic minded, they forget about heaven all together. Both extremes are dangerous and do not serve the Christian faith well. This is surely not what the Bible teach, and it is not what our Lord wants. Let's explore these two groups briefly.

A WORKING VACATION IN HEAVEN?

Heavenly Minded but No Earthly Good

Being heavenly minded is a good thing. The Bible teaches that we should live with eternity in view. Jesus exhorts his followers to "seek first the kingdom of heaven and his righteousness…" (Matthew 6:33). The business and lifestyle of the kingdom should be the priority of the people of God. This was the priority of Jesus and His ministry. Jesus further exhorts us not to store up treasures on earth where we are at risk of losing them and where they have no eternal values. Instead, do our banking in heaven where it is safe (vv.19-24).

Yet, Jesus is not against His followers owning things material or against them planning for tomorrow, prospering, flourishing, and doing well in this world. After all, He created and owns the material world (Psalms 24:1; John 1:1-2). He wants us to live balanced lives, caring for the earth, making a decent living, and keeping eternity in view.

There are Christians who are so enthused and preoccupied about going to heaven, that they live as though they have no responsibility toward this world. In their minds and attitudes, they abandon this world, leaving it for others to care for. Their theme song is "this world is not my home; I am just passing through." These are some of the same people who deny the science of climate change and global warming.

They fail to understand that God gave us the earth to care for it, not to exploit and abuse it (Genesis 1:27-30; Psalm 8:3-8). Christian stewardship responsibility for the earth has not been taught in most churches for decades. The irony is, the

ASSIGNED TO REIGN ON EARTH WITH CHRIST

heaven we are preoccupied with was not given to us; that is God's abode, but for some reason we can't wait to get there.

The opposing position is that of being extremely secular and materialistic. The people who embrace this extreme position, make no room for the spiritual, and that leaves them completely myopic to the eternal; "the god of this world (Satan) has blinded the eyes" of the unbeliever that they cannot see or appreciate things spiritual (2 Corinthians 4:4).

Jesus illustrated this secular position with two stories: 1) the Rich Fool (Luke 12:13-21), and 2) the Rich man and Lazarus (Luke 16:19-31). The first story is about a successful businessman. He acquired his wealth through farming. His farm produced harvest so great, his storage facilities could not contain it. He said to himself, "I am going to tear down my barns and build bigger ones, and I am going to store up much goods for years, and I am going to say to my soul relax and eat, for you have goods for many years" (Luke 12:13-21).

But that very night death came knocking at his door to claim his soul. Now who will get all those goods he has stored up! Why did the Lord call him a fool?

The Lord did not call him a fool because he was rich. The farmer became rich because he was a hard worker and a visionary businessman. The Lord labels him a fool because he had no place in his life for things spiritual. His life was just about him and his business. The message the Lord is getting across is in verse 21: "This is how it will be with whoever stores up things for themselves but is not rich toward God."

A WORKING VACATION IN HEAVEN?

If all you live for is the material, you are a fool, because death can come calling at high noon and you cannot take any of your earthly wealth with you. We must live not neglecting the spiritual aspect of life or taking our eyes off eternity.

The second story has to do with a very rich man and a poor beggar named, Lazarus. The poor man was disabled and had to beg for a living. He was dropped off each day in front of this gated mansion that the rich owner was sure to see him, and hopefully provide some help. The beggar would have been happy with the crumbs that fell from the rich man's table. But not even that much did the rich man allow. He was disgusted seeing him at his gates. The neighborhood dogs had more pit because they licked the beggar's sores.

Well, it so happened that the rich man died and was buried; no doubt had a sumptuous funeral in keeping with his rich lifestyle. He had important people giving speeches about how great he was, and others sent him flowers galore. About the same time the beggar also died, and his soul was carried by angels to Paradise. No burial is indicated. Perhaps his body was just discarded on the city dump for burning. But that is not the end of these two men!

The poor man was carried off by angels to paradise where he was comforted in the afterlife. The rich man was buried, and he went to hell. From there he cried out for mercy! He lived without compassion. The man who had no mercy ended up in hell crying out for mercy (Luke 16:13-31).

ASSIGNED TO REIGN ON EARTH WITH CHRIST

Jesus said, "Blessed are the merciful for they shall obtain mercy" (Matthew 5:7 KJV). The rich man lived a one-sided life, materialistic, and without eternity in view. He could have had the best of both worlds. But he lost everything.

God wants us to live in balance, care for each other and care for the precious earth He gave us. He wants us to enjoy life and keep eternity in our gaze. God's vision is to combine both worlds, heaven, and earth. It is for that reason Jesus taught us to pray, "Thy kingdom come thy will be done on earth as it is in heaven" (Matthew 6:9).The people of God will experience the answer to this prayer because they are the people of the kingdom.

Believers Will Reign on the Earth

Jesus will return to reign on and over the earth as promised, and the people of God will reign on and over the earth with him. How do we know that? The Word of God has made this abundantly clear in numerous passages in both Testaments.

For example, Jude (verse 14) quoted a prophecy by Enoch concerning the Lord coming with thousands upon thousands of His saints. The quote is from a non-canonical source (1Enoch 1:9) but that does not render it without value. Most of the Old Testament (OT) prophets speak of the coming of the Lord with reference to both His first and second advents (e.g., Isaiah 40, 63, 65; Ezekiel 37,38,39; Daniel 12).

Jesus speaks extensively of the coming of the kingdom and of His people inheriting the earth, the kingdom, and

A WORKING VACATION IN HEAVEN?

reigning with Him. Twice in the Beatitudes, reference is made to this: "Blessed are the poor in spirit for theirs is the kingdom of heaven." "Blessed are the meek for they shall inherit the earth" (Matthew 5:3,5). And "Blessed are they that are persecuted for righteousness' sake, for theirs is the kingdom of heaven" (verse 10). The message of the four Gospels and the Epistles is about the kingdom of God and how the people of God will reign with Jesus Christ.

In the apocalypse of John (Revelation 1:5-6), Jesus is identified as "the faithful witness, the firstborn from the dead, and the ruler of the kings of the earth." Who are the kings of the earth? They are the people of God, the ones redeemed out of every nation and language; they will reign with Jesus upon the earth (5:9-10). These people are awarded with crowns and other leadership titles and symbols at the *Believers' Judgment* for their faithful life of service to Christ, and now they return with Him to rule upon and over the earth.

Revelation 19 depicts the people of God in heaven celebrating with Jesus Christ at the marriage supper of the Lamb (verses 9-10). This same crowd is again seen leaving heaven, returning to earth with Jesus on white horses (verses 11-15). Jesus is decorated with the titles KING of Kings and LORD of Lords with many crowns on His head (verse 16). This means He returns to rule but not alone. There are many Kings and Lords that will reign under His administration on earth for a thousand years (Revelation 20:1-6). This is what is referred to as the *Millennium*.

ASSIGNED TO REIGN ON EARTH WITH CHRIST

Jesus returns to earth in the posture of war. This is symbolized by Him riding a white horse with a sharp sword protruding from His mouth. The sword is used to strike down opposing nations. The sword is His word! The word of God is both a creative tool and a weapon (Genesis 1:1-26; Ephesians 6:17; Hebrews 4:12). God brought things into being with His word and will end their existence with His word (2 Peter 3:5-7).

Because of war and the constant threat of nuclear annihilation, some people asked, will there be any earth left to rule over when Jesus returns? The question is posed with the assumption that humans will eventually destroy themselves and the earth. That is the sobering reality world leaders are faced with today. The great nation States possess enough nuclear warheads to destroy the earth many times over. Despite that reality, those of us who know the Word of God are confident God will not allow that for three main reasons.

First, there is the faithfulness of God; it is foundational to both Old and New Testament, the written word of God. Numerous passages speak of the faithfulness of God (Deuteronomy 7:9; 1Corinthians 1:9). Faithfulness is one of the moral attributes of God; it speaks to His trustworthy and righteous character, and the reliability of His Word. His Word must come to pass; it cannot fall to the ground.

Every word of God carries purpose; it is a seed with a mission, and it must grow and come to fruition. Isaiah sums up God's perspective as follows:

A WORKING VACATION IN HEAVEN?

> As the rain and the snow come down from heaven, and do not return to it without watering the earth and making it bud and flourish, so that it yields seed for the sower and bread for the eater, so is my word that goes out from my mouth. It will not return to me empty but will accomplish what I desire and achieve the purpose for which I sent it. (Isiah 55:10-11)

Because of His moral character, God is a covenant making and covenant keeping; He is a promise keeper. His written word to us is a book compiled under two major covenants, Old and New Testament. God is bound to His word.

The second reason humans will not be able to destroy the earth is that God has a purpose for it and that purpose must be fulfilled. Third, God is the Creator of the heavens and the earth. He upholds them by His powerful word, and by the word He sustains them, providentially. God and God alone determines when to replace the present heavens and earth for something new and better (Revelation 21-22).

The Millennial Reign of Christ

The reign of Jesus Christ over the earth is referred to in the literature as the millennium. The word comes from Lattin, *mille annus,* which means a thousand years. It represents a thousand years of peace and prosperity on the earth under the

ASSIGNED TO REIGN ON EARTH WITH CHRIST

Kingship administration of Jesus Christ and His followers. This teaching is largely found in the book of Revelation (20:1-10) but also supported in the Old Testament as a time of peace, prosperity, and freedom from war (Isaiah 9:4-7,11:6-9).

Satan will be in custody during this thousand-year reign of Christ on earth from Jerusalem. The details can be found in my book *Millennium: A Thousand Years of Peace and Prosperity,* in the series "Related Events to the Second Coming of the Christ" (volume 7).[1]

The millennium begins after the Armageddon war in which Jesus defeats the final Gentile powers and rescues Israel from annihilation. The nations are judged and Jesus marches into Jerusalem to sit on the throne of King David to rule over the earth in fulfillment of prophecy (Isaiah 9:6-7). This is the time that the kingdom is restored to Israel that the disciples requested during Jesus' first advent (Acts 1:6-8).

The vast multitude that return to earth with Jesus will serve under various leadership titles over the nations, cities, and towns worldwide. Each nation is ruled by a king to whom all the other leaders report. The Kings, governors, and Lords will all report to the KING of King and LORD of Lord whose throne will be in Jerusalem.

Bear in mind that the vast, diverse multitudes that return from heaven with Jesus will serve in His administration, and they will all be in spiritual bodies that do not get sick or die anymore. Their bodies will be like the resurrection body of Jesus Christ (1John 3:1-3). The people in this category will not be angels but will be like the angels since they will not be married and engaged in procreation (Luke 20:29-36).

But there is a second group of people that did not go to heaven or experience body transformation. This group stayed on earth and survived the Great Tribulation without taking the mark of the beast. They are given the right of passage to enter the millennial kingdom of the Christ. This group will be in their ordinary physical bodies. They will marry, raise a family, and enjoy the peace and prosperity of the millennial kingdom. Jerusalem will be the capital of the earth.

All the people that enter the millennium are followers of Jesus Christ. But the children that are born during this time must accept Jesus as Savior and Lord as we do now. Some will and some will not. The ones that reject Jesus and serve Satan will be numerous but not likely to be in the majority.

If count a generation as 25 years, there will be forty new generations born during the millennium, and not all will accept Jesus. This is why Satan will be released from prison for a short time to organize those who follow him, and they will all face the judgment of God (again see volume 7, The Millennium and volume 9, *The Final Judgment*).

The Reign of Christ and His People

The reign of Christ can be classified in four phases. ***Phase one*:** The Second Person of the blessed Holy Trinity reigns in His preincarnate state as the Word from eternity past to His incarnation in time (John 1:1-7, 14; Philippians 2:5-8).

ASSIGNED TO REIGN ON EARTH WITH CHRIST

Phase two: Runs from His birth to His death. Jesus made it clear to the Pilate, the Roman governor that He is a King, but His kingdom is not of this world (John 18:36-37). Pilate new then that Jesus pose no threat to Ceasar and declared Him innocent, finding no charge against Him (verses 38-39).

Phase three: The third stage of Jesus' kingship began with His resurrection, ascension, and exaltation to the right hand of the Father. Philippians (2:9-11) tells us that God exalted His Son to the "highest place and gave him the name that is above every name, that at the name of Jesus every knee will bow...and every tongue confess that Jesus Christ is Lord to the glory of God the Father."

This wholesale submission to the authority of Christ will not happen in the earth realm until His second advent of the Christ when every nation, even Israel that rejected Him, will now embrace Him as their Messiah, Lord, and Savior. The third phase of His kinship, therefore, will continue throughout the millennium to the end of the Final Judgment when all oppositions are forever vanquished from His creation (Revelation 20:11-13).

All through the millennium to the end of the Final Judgment, the people of God will be reigning with Christ upon and over the earth. They will even assist Christ at Final Judgment. The apostle Paul declares, "do you not know that the Lord's people will judge the world? Do you not know we will judge angels? How much more the things of this life!" (1Corinthians 6:1-4).

A WORKING VACATION IN HEAVEN?

Phase four: The fourth phase of Christ Kingship reign is His joint reign with the Father in the New World order into eternity future.[2] We will speak more of this fourth phase in the next chapter.

Summary

In this chapter we set out to show that the people of God taken to heaven at the rapture, will return to earth to live and reign with Jesus Christ for a thousand years. This period is called the millennium. This means our stay in heaven will be a short stay of only seven years, the duration of the Great Tribulation. In fact, our stay in heaven will be a working vacation.

We will return to reign upon and over the earth with Jesus Christ. Upon His return to earth, Jesus will take over the administration of government in fulfillment of the following prophecy:

> For to us a child is born, to us a son is given, and the government will be upon his shoulders. And he will be called, Wonderful Counselor, Mighty God, Everlasting Father, Prince. Of the greatness of his government and peace there will be no end. He will reign on David's throne and over his kingdom, establishing and upholding it with justice and righteousness from that time on and forever. The zeal of the LORD Almighty will accomplish this. (Isaiah 9:6-7)

ASSIGNED TO REIGN ON EARTH WITH CHRIST

This is the first time Jesus will sit on a throne on earth as the head of government. His people will be fully in charge of His administration. This truth counters the popular view of going to heaven to live and reign permanently with Jesus.

Upon returning to earth from our rendezvous in heaven, we are put to work in the administration of Jesus Christ over the earth. We will remain in charge to the end of the millennium and the final judgment. During that time many of us will be Kings and Priest, Lords, and Governors, among other titled positions over countries, cities, and towns all over the world. So, there will be peace on earth as the angelic choir sang on the night of His birth to shepherds on a Judean hill. And all the covenant promises made to Israel will be fulfilled.

For us, the people of God, reigning with Christ over this old earth will be the first phase of our kingly reign with Jesus Christ. But like everything else, this too will end. The next chapter begins the second phase of our reign with Christ.

A WORKING VACATION IN HEAVEN?

CHAPTER 4

THE ETERNAL REIGN OF THE SON OF GOD

In the preceding chapter, the reign of Christ and His people over the present earth have come to an end. The earth and the heavens have also ended. They are demolished because they are used, old, and tainted. The end of the present created order is expected because the creation is not eternal; it has a beginning, and it has an end.

Just in case some people did not fully understand that the present creation will come to an end after the *Final Judgment*, let us revisit that scenario briefly. Let us consider four major intelligence reports from scripture that forecast the future of the present creation.

The Future Status of the Present Creation

The first intelligence report is found in Romans 8:18-25. In these verses we find the future hope of the people of God and the creation. The creation is not here by blind, random chance as secular humanism would have us believe, but by the will of God. For convenience, the full text is provided here:

> 18 I consider that our present sufferings are not worth comparing with glory that will be revealed in us. 19 For the creation waits in eager expectations for the children of God. 20 For the creation was subjected to frustration, not by its own choice, but by the will of the one who subjected it, in hope 21 that the creation itself will be liberated from its bondage to decay and brought into the freedom and glory of the children of God.
>
> 22 We know that the whole creation has been groaning as in the pains of childbirth right up to this present time. 23 Not only so, but we ourselves, who have the firstfruits of the Spirit, groan inwardly as we wait eagerly for

> our adoption to sonship, the redemption of our bodies. 24 For in this hope we were saved. But hope that is seen is no hope at all. Who hope for what they already have? 25 But if we hope for what we do not yet have, we wait for it patiently. (Romans 8:18-26)

There are three lessons to highlight from the preceding quote. ***First***, like us humans, the creation has fallen from its original glory, purpose, and pristine state, and is undergoing decay and death. And just as humans experience suffering and pain as part of the dying process, the creation is suffering the same (Romans 8:22). Because of the Fall of man, a curse was place on the earth (Genesis 3:17-19).

Second, unlike humans, the creation did not by its own choice subjected itself to decay and death. God did it, but in hope of a future deliverance from decay and death (Genesis 3:20-21). Our ancestral parents sinned by choice in Eden.

Third, just as humans (e.g., the people of God) are going through rebirth and transformation, leading to glorification, the rest of creation will also go through a transformation and glorification (Romans 8:23). In view of this change, the apostle Paul declares, "Therefore, if anyone is in Christ, he is a new creation. The old has passed away; behold, the new has come" (2 Corinthians 5:17 ESV).

For the people of God, this process of change begins with the new birth, being born again, and will culminate in resurrection and glorification of our bodies (John 3:5-8, 5:28;

A WORKING VACATION IN HEAVEN?

Romans 8:28-30). For us therefore, life is not meaningless; it is the unfolding of God's creation plan. He orders it!

The second intelligence report is Hebrews (1:10-12). This report affirms that the present created order is decaying and will ultimately perish. The following scripture text also confirms the immutability, indestructability, and eternality of the Creator God Himself.

> In the beginning, Lord, you laid the foundations of the earth, and the heavens are the work of your hands. They will perish, but you remain; they will wear out like a garment. You will roll them up like a robe; like a garment they will be changed. But you remain the same, and your years will never end. (Hebrews 1:10-12 NIV)

It is clear from the preceding quote that the creation is decaying and will eventually perish, and discorded. Creation has a shelf-life, and scientists have uncovered that fact; it is called "entropy" (https://en.wikipedia.org/wiki/Entropy).

The scripture quote goes on to affirm the eternal and unchanging nature of the Son of God who Himself is the agent of creation (John 1:1-4; Colossians 1:15-17). The Son always exist. He is not aging, and He cannot perish, therefore, He is well able to destroy and create all things new as He sees fit.

The third intelligence report concerning the future of the present creation (2 Peter 3: 2-7). Here is the full text:

THE ETERNAL REIGN OF THE SON OF GOD

> 2 I want you to recall the words spoken in the past by the holy prophets and the command given by our Lord and Savior through your apostles. 3 Above all, you must understand that in the last days scoffers will come, scoffing and following their own evil desires. 4 They will say, "Where is this coming, he promised? Ever since our ancestors died, everything goes on as it has since the beginning of creation." 5 But they deliberately forget that long ago by God's word the heavens came into being and the earth was formed out of water and by water. 6 By these waters also the world of that time was deluged and destroyed. 7 By the same word the present heavens and earth are reserved for fire, being kept for the day of judgment and destruction of the ungodly. (2 Peter 3:2-7)

The God who created the earth told Noah He was going to destroy everything and start over, and He did. The same God told Abraham that the morality of Sodom and Gomorrah stunk to high heaven, and He was going to clean it up by fire, and He did (Genesis 18-19).

Now, the same God who created heavens and earth is telling us there is an expiration date, a shelf-life to the present creation and He will replace them with better and newer versions. But some of His human tenants scoffed, telling us it won't happen; the earth has always been here, and it will continue to be here, they say.

But the people of God do not consider the warning a laughing matter. We know what is coming is certain, that Jesus will do away with the old order to bring in the new before He commences His eternal reign. We are in the last of the last days, so the next bulletin is the final forecast the Creator has given about the future of the creation.

The fourth intelligence report is Revelation 20:11-15. This passage records for us the countdown to the end of the old, created order. It includes all the bad things that spoil a once pristine creation: sin, Satan and his angels, wicked humans, death, hades, old earth, and old heaven—all will perish as the Hebrew 1:10-12 passage tells us.

Revelation 21 opens with three new things: 1) a new heaven, 2) a new earth, and 3) the New Jerusalem. The new Jerusalem is the new eternal capital of the new heaven and earth. For details see my book, *The New World Order* (Vol.10) in the series, "Related Events to the Second Coming of the Christ." As stated in the introduction, this work is supplemental to that series, making more robust some points that were glossed over on purpose.

The Eternal Reign of the Christ

THE ETERNAL REIGN OF THE SON OF GOD

The second person of the blessed Holy Trinity has always been King and will always be King. But for the purpose of this study, I have chosen to divide His Kingship into four stages, as shown earlier.

The first stage is *His Pre-incarnate Kingship*. It runs from eternity past (dateless past) to His incarnation as the Son of Man, Jesus Nazareth, the Christ. The name designated to the Son of God during His pre-incarnate existence is the eternal Word, the Logos (John 1:1-7, 14; Philippians 2:5-7).

The second stage is *His Incarnate Kingship* runs from His birth in Bethlehem of Judea to His death on the cross. It covers His earthly existence in the physical body, His pre-resurrection life. Jesus never sat on any earthly throne, but He never denied that He was a King whose kingdom is not of this world (Matthew 2:1-12; John 18:33-37).

The third stage is *His Post-resurrection Kingship* which runs from His resurrection, ascension, exaltation to the right hand of the Father through to the end of the millennium, and the final judgment. The Final Judgment culminates with the end of the old-world order as we know it. By then Jesus would have put down and sweep away all opposing powers to His authority to the glory of God the Father (Philippians 2:9-11).

This is so because to the end of the millennium, Satan will have diehard human followers who refuse to acknowledge the authority of Jesus Christ. They will defy Him even though He is literally sitting on the throne of David ruling over the earth from Jerusalem.

A WORKING VACATION IN HEAVEN?

For this reason, among others, Satan will be loosed from prison to marshal his followers in one last attempt to overthrow Jesus Christ; at that time, they will be forced to acknowledge His authority when fire comes down from heaven and devour Satan's human followers.

Later, they will then be resurrected, judged, and thrown into the eternal lake of burning sulfur, otherwise known as hell (Revelation 20:7-15). Satan is already Judged but won't be sentenced until then (John 16:11). He is also thrown in the lake of burning sulfur. Everyone gets a body suitable to their eternal destination (see volume 8 *Resurrection of Humans*).

The fourth phase is the *Kingship of His Eternal Reign with the Father*. This phase begins with the New World Order to eternity future (dateless future without end). I did promise to return to this fourth phase later, because it needs a little unpacking. Well, this is it, So, let's get to it!

In his resurrection discourse of First Corinthians 15, the apostle Paul gives us the following insightful revelation about the nature of the eternal Kingship of the Son of God:

> Then comes the end, when He delivers the kingdom to God the Father, when He puts an end to all rule and all authority and power. For He must reign till He has put all enemies under His feet. The last enemy that will be destroyed is death. (1Corinthians 15:24-26 NKJV)

THE ETERNAL REIGN OF THE SON OF GOD

The preceding quote is fulfilled with the end of the old-world order as Revelation (20:11-15) has shown. There is no more opposing authority to the authority of Jesus Christ after the final judgment. The final enemy, death, is destroyed; it has no more usefulness. So, the kingdom is handed over to God the Father by the Son. The administration of God is back to what it was in the pre-incarnate state of the Son; the Father, Son, Holy Spirit rule as one God.

The Holy Spirit is not mentioned in this scripture citation; it shows the Father and the Son ruling jointly from their new residence, the New Jerusalem (Revelation 22:3). But we know from Scripture that the Holy Trinity is inseparable. Jesus is ruling jointly with the Father after this handoff, but there are some noted differences.

First, there is a new heaven and a new earth because all things are created new as already discussed (Revelation 21).

Second, the incarnation has produced for God sons and daughters He never had before; these are the people of God. This is what God intended when He created Adam and Eve. He intended to populate the earth with righteous people who would be His family. But His family was highjacked by another spirit being who wanted a family of his own.

The Fall of man corrupted the seed of mankind, making it possible for Satan to build a family of his own. The New Testament has much to say about the children of God and the children of the evil One. Cain was Satan's child (Genesis 4: 6-16; 1John 3:10-12).

A WORKING VACATION IN HEAVEN?

Satan has spiritual paternity over some humans. Jesus said to a group of religious people, "You are of your father the devil, and the desires of your father you want to do. He was a murderer from the beginning" (John 8:44). Redemption is God's plan to rescue His family through a new birth experience in Jesus Christ (John 3:5, 16; Ephesian 2:1-7).

We who are born again into the kingdom of God are the children of God from both Old and New Testament. We were both redeemed by the work of Christ on the cross, that in the ages to come, we could showcase the riches of God's grace (Ephesians 2:7). We will first showcase God's grace in this world during Church Age, the Millennial Age, and then the ages to come; that is eternity future, which begins when Jesus hands off the kingdom to the Father.

Third, God has relocated His new residence to be closer to the new earth. It will be closer than the old heaven was to the old earth. This is done so that God can dwell with people, His new and expanded family (Revelation 21:1-4).

In the old order, God's dwelling place was the third heaven, that's the place we were raptured to, and spent seven years before we returned to the old earth to reign with Christ in the millennium. In the new order, God's dwelling place is close to the new earth.

Fourth, heaven and earth are now connected (Revelation 21:1-21). This is the full blown "thy kingdom come, thy will be done on earth as it is in heaven" that we have been praying for during the Church Age in the Lord's prayer (Matt.6:9-10).

THE ETERNAL REIGN OF THE SON OF GOD

Bible scholars believe that the New Jerusalem will be suspended over the new earth and is accessible from the four regions of the earth through twelve gates that are never closed (21: 9-21). They are opened because there are no nefarious intruders; nonetheless, angels guard them (verse 12).

Each region of the new earth has three gates to access the capital city, the New Jerusalem. During the millennial reign of Christ over the old earth, He reigns from Jerusalem in Israel, and the kings of the earth travel there yearly to pay him homage (Isaiah 9:6-7). But now He is reigning from the New Jerusalem, and the dwellers of the new earth have free and open access to God. He dwells among His people in the New Jerusalem. His people can see His face without dying (Revelation 22:1-5).

Summary

This chapter deals with the Kingship reign of the Son of God in four stages: His pre-incarnate reign, His incarnate reign, His post-resurrection reign, and His future eternal reign with His people. Much of what is to come is not yet revealed. Therefore, we can only speak of that which is revealed, the secret things belong to God, as such, they are classified.

But this one thing we know, our God and His Christ, and the blessed Holy Spirit will rule for all eternity with His extended family. We have every confidence that all will be well. For us humans the sacrifice of the Lamb of God for our

A WORKING VACATION IN HEAVEN?

redemption has paid-off our sin debt in full, and for that reason, we have an eternally bright future.

CHAPTER 5

THE ETERNAL REIGN OF GOD'S PEOPLE

We have only a faint knowledge of what the eternal reign of the Son of God will be like; we know from where He will be ruling and we know His rule is eternal. But eyes have not seen, and ears have not heard, and hearts and minds have not perceived the length and scope of what God has planned for those He loves and those who love Him. Revelation 21 and 22 give us a sweeping and awe-inspiring vision of what is to come, but much remain classified.

A WORKING VACATION IN HEAVEN?

Let's be more direct about the people of God. What will our reign be like, and from where will we be ruling, and for how long? This chapter tries to look behind the curtains for what revelation knowledge we can glean to answer these three questions. We will answer the last question first.

How Long Is Our Reign?

The reign of the people of God will be eternal. The word "eternal" has at least two meanings. When used in reference to God (i.e., any member of the Holy Trinity), it means infinite, having no beginning and having no end. God owes His existence to no one outside of Himself because He is self-existent. God has life within Himself (John 5:26-27).

When "eternal" is used in reference to created beings, such as angels and humans, it means having a beginning existence but no end. Humans have a physical body that dies, but the human consciousness or spirit or soul continues to live and will be given a new body at the resurrection (John 5:28).

Eternal life is not only longevity of life, but quality of life, life in its fullness. Jesus promised His people fullness of life, that fullness begins with the new birth and continues to unfold from glory to glory (John 10:10b).

Again, created things below angels and humans have no ontological status, so they are not eternal. They have a beginning, and they all have an end. Therefore, the plant kingdom and the animal kingdom are not eternal in any sense of the word or the cosmos itself. I referred to the law of entropy earlier; it reminds us that the whole creation is running down or dying. Humans are destined for glorification.

The words eternal life, of course, needs further unpacking because it is often a misunderstood term. A person can only reign eternally if he or she has accepted the offer of eternal life (John 3:16). Though offered to all humankind, it appears, only a small group will respond positively to the offer; possibly a few billion, when compared to the billions that have lived. Some will ask, how do I come to this conclusion?

Speaking of those who respond to the offer of eternal life, Jesus said, "...narrow is the gate and difficult is the Way which leads to life, and there are few who find it" (Matthew 7:13 NKJV). It is not that the path is hidden, but the lifestyle is not attractive. Or the offer sounds too good to be true, so some people reject it on that premise.

Eternal life is given the moment a person is born again into the kingdom of God (John 3:5). But bear in mind that eternal life is only resident in Jesus Christ (John 3:14-18). You cannot bypass Jesus Christ and still receive eternal life. Think about it! Some people say, we are Abraham's seed, we are chosen by God. That is only true if they embrace Yeshua as the Messiah (John 1:12).

Jesus is God's gift to the world, that is to all humankind, not just to church folks or any special ethnic group. The Word of God is clear, "For God so loved the world that he gave his one and only Son, that whoever believes in him shall not perish but have eternal life" (John 3:16). Let me emphasize,

A WORKING VACATION IN HEAVEN?

eternal life is God's gift to all humans. The apostle Paul writes, "[The penalty] for sin is death, but the gift of God is eternal life through Jesus Christ out Lord" (Romans 6:23).

This gift is only offered through the person Jesus Christ; there is no other name under heaven eternal life is possible (Acts 4:12; Romans 5:1-8). Religion without Jesus Christ, the Son of God, does not offer eternal life. Therefore, if the gift is not accepted, it is rejected, and the person who rejects God's gift of salvation in Jesus Christ will perish (John 3:16). Put bluntly, that person is forever lost.

Immediately after death, that person will find himself in a place of torment (Luke 16:19-31). And he will be later called from that place of torment to face judgment, and be sentenced to hell, the lake of burning sulfur (Revelation 20:11-15).

Some people mistakenly think eternal life is given after physical death. But if you wait until you are dead, you have lost your chance, and there is not a second chance. Eternal life must be received while you are alive in your physical body; it must be a present possession (John 4:13-14, 5:24, 10:27-28).

What does eternal life mean? It means life without limit; lift without deficit: no sickness, no disease, no death or lack. It is life from fullness to fullness or from glory to glory in a perfect environment forever. Those who reject the offer of eternal life will experience eternal death, an unimaginable existence of endless torment without God. So, to answer the question, how long the righteous will reign? They will reign forever and ever, eternally.

THE ETERNAL REIGN OF GOS'S PEOPLE

Where and Over What Will the People of God Reign?

The Bible tells us, we will inherit the earth, reign upon the earth, rule over a kingdom sitting on thrones (Matthew 5:5,10 19:28-30). But for some reason, we gloss over these verses and fix our gaze on another realm called heaven. But God created the earth for a purpose, and He will recreate it for a purpose. So, we will reign upon the earth (Revelation 5:10).

First, during the millennial reign of the Christ, the people of God will reign on and over the present earth under the Kingship of Jesus Christ. Jesus at that time will be ruling from earthly Jerusalem in Israel, where He sits on the throne of David in fulfillment of prophecies and promises made to His ancient people (Isaiah 9:6-7). That phase of Christ's reign and the believers' reign will end after the *Final Judgment*.[1]

Second, Christ and His people will transition to reign from and over the New Jerusalem and over the new earth. As indicated in the previous chapter, God the Father and His Son, and of course the blessed Holy Spirit, will be reigning jointly over the universe, which includes the new heaven, and the new earth. The seat of government will be in the New Jerusalem, the universal capital city (Revelation 21:1-8).

Scholars believe this heavenly City of God will be suspended over the new earth. It is a massive city with twelve foundations, unlike anything seen by humans in the old world. It surpasses in splendor, beauty, and luxury any city of man.[2]

Our current levels of technology and physics make it difficult to imagine the reality of such a city. For that reason,

A WORKING VACATION IN HEAVEN?

some scholars are more inclined to think of the twelve foundations in symbolic terms. The difficulty conceptualizing a twelve-foundation city lies in our finite, fallen condition. Furthermore, our current world is four-dimensional, and such architecture would require more than the four dimensions we currently know and have grown accustomed to.

We function in a world with three spatial dimensions of length, width, and height. We navigate this world in forward and backward (East and West), upward and downward (North and South) movements (spatial). But note that we use time to navigate our world, so Albert Einstein added the fourth dimension known as "spacetime."[3] Scientists believe there might be up to ten dimensions available, but we have not yet learned the physics and technologies to access them.[4]

Therefore, since God created all dimensions and is capable of dwelling in all of them, it is presumptuous to say, He cannot build such a city with twelve or more foundations. God is omnipotent and infinite, omniscient, omnipresent, and eternal. To put limits on Him is to create a god in our own image and likeness, which would not be the God of the Bible.

The New Jerusalem comes down from God out of heaven, where it was built not by humans, so its architecture would transcend what we now know in our finite state. The city described in Revelation, chapters 21 and 22, is believed to be shaped like a cube with six sides. And it is possible to build structures on all six sides once the gravity problem is resolved.[5]

THE ETERNAL REIGN OF GOS'S PEOPLE

From our current understanding, buildings on the underside would appear to be upside down. Such construction would defy current technology and physics.[6] But that is expected because it is not a city conceived and constructed by humans, so anything is possible. Millions, if not billions of glorified humans will live and frequently visit this city.

Third, the people of God will be living in both the capital city and on the new earth; they will be ruling from and over both under the Kinship of the Father, Son, and Holy Spirit. We do not know now what criteria God will use to assign new earth dwellers and new Jerusalem dwellers.

Perhaps, the people who rule over what we call nations, but the Bible refers to as kingdoms, will dwell on the earth, while those who administer the affairs of the capital city will dwell in the capital city. The word of God makes it clear that the people of God will rule over kingdoms and for that reason many are given crowns which are symbols of head leadership.

But there are many other titles under kings. Believers are called the kings of the earth because they will reign under Jesus Christ, the KING of Kings and LORD of Lords (Revelation 19:16). As stated before, the capital city is believed to suspend over the new earth with constant and seamless accessibility though the twelve gates that never closed. The new earth and the capital city appear to function as one unit. God dwelling with His people, a complete fulfillment of the line in the Lord's prayer, "thy Kingdom

A WORKING VACATION IN HEAVEN?

come, thy will be done on earth as it is in heaven" (Matthew 6:10 KJV).

There are those who see Israel and the Church as two separate people. But from the gospel Jesus intended Gentiles and Israel to be one flock, in one sheepfold, under one shepherd (John 10:1-29). In this context some scholars see the Church as the bride of Christ and is distinct and separate from Israel for all eternity. But bear in mind that God did marry Israel at Sinai as His covenant people. The fact is—marriage is used symbolically to define God's relationship with His people Israel and the Church. But in fact, they are one people.

Furthermore, throughout the Epistles, Paul and the other apostles kept hammering home that in Christ we are all one body. There neither male are female, Jew or Gentile, bond or free (Ephesians 2:11-22). The mystery of uniting Jews and Gentiles, heaven and earth in one body in Christ was first made known to Paul (Colossians 1:25-27).

Others argue that since the Church is the Bride of Christ, the Bride will always be with the Groom. But again, this is a misunderstanding of scripture. The Bride and Groom scenario is symbolic of the intimate relationship between Christ and His people (Ephesian 5:21-33). There is no other relationship on earth to illustrate this lasting, intimate union besides marriage. But it should not be taken as marriage as we know marriage, but like a marriage. It is a figure of speech.

Jesus Himself said in heaven people will not be married or given to marriage; they will be like the angels (Matthew

THE ETERNAL REIGN OF GOS'S PEOPLE

22:23-30). Jesus then would be the lead example. For more on this see my book, *The Coronation the Christ*...in the series, "Related Events to the Second Coming of the Christ").[7]

If the twelve foundations of the capital city are taken literally, and there is no reason they should not be, then the accommodations will exceed the population of twelve of the largest cities on the old earth combined. The earthly Jerusalem had twelve gates to give it ease of accessibility. For the same reason, the New Jerusalem has twelve gates, each is named for the twelve tribes of Israel.

The foundations are named for the twelve apostles of the Lamb. Yet this is one massive city for the people of God, under the administration of one God.

Summary

This chapter answers three questions: how long the people of God will reign, where will they reign from, and over what will they reign? We are unable to answer every detail because much of the information about *the new world order* remain classified. But God has revealed enough to give us a limited, yet awe-inspiring preview.

The Scriptures teach that eternal life is gifted to live and rule in a kingdom that never ends. But eternal life is much more than longevity of life, it is also qualitative life, life in the highest, fullest form in a progressive, perfect environment.

A WORKING VACATION IN HEAVEN?

The people of God will first rule upon and over the earth during the millennial reign of the Christ. Then after the final judgment, they will transition to occupy and reign on and over the new earth and the New Jerusalem.

Indeed, eyes have not yet seen, and ears have not heard, or have it entered into the hearts of humans or conceived with the mind the fullness of what God has prepared for them that love Him. We cannot be stubbornly dogmatic on some things because the full information is classified. We do not know! Bu the things that are reveled give us a good picture of things to come. For the people of God, that is, those who have put their faith in Jesus Christ, the unfolding of the future is bright and flourishing.

CHAPTER 6

THE GOD KIND OF LIFE
Part 1

Setting the Context

The kind of life God desires for humankind now and for eternity can be summarized under six objective, and transcendent values: holiness, love, righteousness, truth, justice, and mercy. Note these six values because we will be discussing them from now to the end of this book. We will cover three in this chapter, and the other three in chapter 7.

I refer to these six values as "objective and transcendent values" because they came down from God to us, not

A WORKING VACATION IN HEAVEN?

ascended from us to God. God used these values to speak of Himself and to set the standard He requires of us humans to conform. We are the ones who are being shaped into the image of God through Christ, not the other way around (Romans 12:1-2). Some humans are trying to make God into their own image and likeness, but that is an exercise in futility.

If each of us defines these words to meet our individual situation, then we are providing multiple subjective meanings to each word and transferring them to God. Our meanings would be generally contrary to God's meaning. Plus, they would be situational and pragmatic, putting personal needs at the center. God wants us to be holy because He is holy, loving because He is love, and truthful because He is truth. We should always exercise these values, even when doing so hurts our personal interests and go contrary to our personal desires.

But if God by His word tells us what He means by these values, all we need to do is adjust our behavior to what is said. His definition drives the conforming behavior. For example, if God said, do not eat the fruit of the tree in the middle of the garden, because you will be corrupted by it, and it will lead to your unhappiness and death. Then holiness to God is my obedience of not eating from the forbidden tree.

God has given His word about that tree. If I intend to live by what God said, then I must adjust my behavior to comply with His word, not what anyone else said about the tree and its fruits. I must conform to—*do not eat*. Had our ancestral

THE GOD KIND OF LIFE - PART 1

parents in the Paradise Garden obeyed the command of God, the world would be a better place today.

It was God who gave His values to Moses in the form of Ten Commandments on Mount Sinai. These laws came down from God out of heaven to humankind on earth, not as suggestions to ignore, but as executive orders to obey. They are divine, transcendent, objective, and behavioral values.

To God, holiness is obeying His laws. God's law keeps me safe from God, from myself, and from my neighbor. If I worship Baal or make images for worship or covet my neighbor's spouse or murder him, these are unholy acts, and I am in trouble with God. The law of God is the word of God; it is intended to protect me from God, from my neighbor, and from myself. Even civil laws protect me from myself, from my neighbor, and from the government.

So then, behavior is something we do, and for the most part, they are observable. The six values given in the first paragraph are to be viewed within this contextual background.

These six values are moral attributes of the divine nature and are essential for humans to be in accord with the divine will and purpose. In other words, God desires humans to possess and express these values in their relationship to Him and in their relationships with neighbors. Why?

Because these values constitute the God kind of life required now for human flourishing on this earth. They also prepare us to live and reign with God on the coming new earth and the New Jerusalem. The people of God begin to live the

God kind of life now in view of eternity. By now, I mean from the time of our new birth, the time we are born again into the kingdom of God and adopted into His family (John 3:5-8;Romans 8:14-17).

Each attribute is extensive enough to fill several large volumes. We will not attempt such encyclopedic task in this small book, but in an introductory way, I will touch upon all six essentials of the spiritual life in Jesus Christ.

I am acutely aware that God cannot be capsulized or squeezed into any one word or phrase, yet all six attributes constitute an essential snapshot of God's moral nature. These attributes are inherent to His character; they are not just what God does; they are what He is. Let's consider each briefly.

The Holiness Attribute

Holiness is the first essential moral attribute of God we encounter in the Torah (the Law). The Law is the first five books of the Hebrew and Christian Bible. Except for a chapter or two, it is commonly accepted that these books were written by the Moses (Genesis, Exodus, Leviticus, Numbers, and Deuteronomy). The information in the Torah came from three major sources: Moses himself, the oral tradition, and divine revelation (i.e., from God Himself). Context is important here.

First, from Moses himself. Moses was the son of Hebrew slaves, born in Egypt. His ancestors are the family of Jacob who settled in Egypt because of a severe famine over the whole land of Cannan and Egypt. But Egypt had food.

THE GOD KIND OF LIFE - PART 1

Moses was born in a time of State sponsored genocide. The Pharaoh issued an executive order to execute all newborn Hebrew males. After Moses was born, he was hidden for a few months. When his parents could hide him no more, they placed him in a basket adrift on the Nile. His parents hoped that someone of means would discover him and save his life. It worked, not by accident or coincidence, but by divine intervention. The whole thing was a human and divine plan.

It so happened that the basket with the child was discovered by Pharaoh's daughter. She had gone to the river to bathe and lo and behold, there was the child a drift in this beautiful basket, which was meticulously constructed. Upon having her servants retrieve the child from the waters, she recognized him as one of the Hebrew babies.

Hiding in the bushes nearby, was the child's sister Miriam, who rushed out and asked, Shall I go and get one of the Hebrew women to a nurse the baby for you? The princess gave permission. Miriam went and called the baby's mother. The princess said, "Take this baby and nurse him for me, and I will pay you." When the child came of age, the princess adopted him as her son (Exodus 2:1-10).

She named him Moses and she raised him as an Egyptian, but the babysitter she hired already taught the child his true identity but kept it a secret. Moses was adopted into royalty and lived at the palace as a Prince of Egypt.

With this privileged upbringing, Moses got the best education and military training as a Prince of Egypt. But he

A WORKING VACATION IN HEAVEN?

had a secret. He dressed and talked like a true Egyptian, but he knew he was the son of Hebrew slaves.

One day, he saw an Egyptian beating a Hebrew, and he angrily tried to break it up, but the Egyptian was killed in the process. He buried him secretly, but a day or two later he discovered others knew about it. His cover as a true Egyptian was blown, so he fled Egypt fearing the wrath of the Pharaoh. He was forty years old at the time. His life of privilege ended.

Moses settled with a desert family in Median. The head of this family was a man named Jethro; he was a priest and a farmer of sheep and goats. Jethro had seven daughters. Moses married one and became part of this family and for the next forty years worked as a shepherd. With all that education and military training, he was raising sheep and goats. If the story ended here, you would say, "how disappointing!"

But it was at that ripe age of eighty that all the pieces came together to fulfil the true purpose of his life. God called and commissioned him to liberate the Israelites from Egypt. There was no better man for this job than Moses. He was educated, had military training as a soldier, the patience of a shepherd to lead, he spoke Hebrew and Egyptian, he knew Egypt and he knew the terrain of the dessert. Sometimes God is preparing us for our big assignment, so be faithful in what you now do.

An educated man would normally keep a journal of all that happened to him and a journal of his family history. When the time came to write the Torah, Moses himself was a rich source of information.

THE GOD KIND OF LIFE - PART 1

Second, the oral tradition. Since only the elite could read and write back then, people told their history in story form. Fathers tell it to their sons and daughters, and they tell it to the generations following (Psalm 44:1-3). This is called the oral tradition. Mose lived 120 years. Think of the many fathers and mothers he had spoken to for their stories, the genealogy records tapped into to learn who begot who, and so on.

Third, God Himself as source. The Bible tells us that Moses spoke to God face to face. He was personally instructed by God, not only for eighty full days (40+40) on Sinai but constantly. Moses was a student under God's tutelage.

Moses wrote about the creation of the world because God revealed it to him. God download His knowledge into Moses and Moses in turn wrote it on scrolls for the instruction of the Hebrew nation and the nations of the world. Why the nations? God intended to populate the whole earth with families, and family of nations. He told Abraham he would be a father of many nations (Genesis 12:1-3).

We are talking about the holiness of God as one of His personal attributes or qualities, but we need to provide context. Now that we have provided that, we can focus more directly on holiness.

The first time we come upon the word "holy" in the Torah is in Exodus (3:5) with Moses at the burning bush. He is tending his father-in-law's sheep in the mountain region of the desert and there he beheld a strange phenomenon, a bush ablaze, yet not consumed by the fire. He turned aside to examine it more closely, and God spoke to him from the blazing bush. The voice said, "Moses! Moses! Do not come any closer, take off your sandals, for the place where you are standing is holy ground" (Exodus 3:5).

What lessons can we draw from this encounter with God as it relates to His Being? I see three: 1) God is holy in His nature and person, 2) wherever God chose to manifest His presence that place is holy, and 3) whoever represents God must be holy; He demands holiness.

From this holy ground encounter of Moses with God, the word holy is frequently repeated throughout the Hebrew and Christian Bible hundreds of times to the last book of the Bible. From the earliest of time, God made it clear that He is holy and anyone or anything associated with Him must be holy. This is implied from the *Paradise Garden*. When Adam and Eve crossed the holiness boundary to sin, the holy glory that covered them departed. Then God judged them for their sinful behavior and expelled them from the garden.

God is holy. The heavenly host repeats it: Holy! Holy! Holy is the Lord God Almighty (Isaiah 6:1-7; Revelation 4:8). Holiness is essential to God's nature, character, and being. His holiness is represented in various expressions such as, "God Most High," which speaks to His transcendence, His wholly otherness. "God is light," which suggests absolute purity, knowledge, and enlightenment. "God is a consuming fire" which reflects His cleansing, purifying power as well as wrath and judgment (Hebrews 12:14-17, 28-29; 1John 1:5-7).

THE GOD KIND OF LIFE - PART 1

This next scripture should be carefully read and contemplated. It is dramatic and terrifying; it gives us insight into the holy character of God. Aaron, Moses' brother and the first high priest of Israel, had two of his sons slain for offering strange fire, unholy fire in worship (Leviticus10:1-11).

But what is the meaning of the word, holy? It means separation from sin and defilements, and dedication to God, cleanness or purity. Human holiness is generally called sanctification. We are called to holiness, which means we must separate ourselves from sin and moral filthiness and dedicate ourselves unto God. But humans cannot do this by themselves alone; they need divine help. That is why there is a human and divine side to sanctification or holiness.

When the repentant sinner comes to God through Jesus Christ, he or she is sanctified by the word of God, by the blood of Jesus Christ, and by the refiner's fire of the blessed Holy Spirit. But that is just the beginning of a long journey or walking in sanctification. There are things that I must do to separate myself from moral filth and dedicate myself to God; it is a process. I must put to death the carnal nature or sinful passions that seek to keep me in chains (Galatians 5:17-21). And I must yield myself to the Holy Spirit to cultivate in me the fruit of the Spirit (Galatians 5: 22-26).

Holiness or sanctification is an event with a lengthy process that spans a believer's entire life in Christ. As a believer, I must give myself daily to God and have my mind spiritually renewed (Romans 12:1-2). The life in Christ is not lived after the flesh or carnal desires. I must crucify those proclivities or passions, put them to death, so I can live a life led by the Spirit of God (Roman 8:5-11).

God intends to rid His creation of all that is unholy, corrupted, and evil; the final judgment will accomplish that (Revelation 20:11-15). But God will not stop there; He will destroy the current created order and create a new heaven and a new earth that are not tainted by sin (Revelation 21:1-5). Only those who are holy will occupy this new heaven, the new earth, and the New Jerusalem (Revelation 21:5-8). The holiness of God will prevail over all creation.

The Attribute of Love

The apostle John writes, "God is love" (1John 4:8). Love is another moral attribute of God; it is essential to His nature. Whatever God does is done in love. He created us in love, and He redeems us in love (John 1:1-5, 3:16).

God is the supreme lover over all, and He wants His love reciprocated. This is evident in the two great works of God: creation and redemption. All things are created for a purpose, and by exercising that purpose they give back. The sea and the land give back to sustain the cycle of life; they are both a source of food and much more. All creation is giving back.

The second great work of God is redemption. In general, redemption is the rescue or buying back of created things, in particular created persons, humankind. Redemption is a work of love for the primary benefit of humans. Love moved God to give His one and only Son (John 3:16; Romans 6:23). But does God expect reciprocation? Does the farmer sow without the expectation of a harvest? Yes, God expects a return.

By giving His Son, God in turn receives many sons and daughters. So, the love of God is reciprocated, though not equally. God's give of love in Jesus Christ is unmatched. He gave the gift of far greater value. Our redemption cost God the life of His Son. It is the supreme act of love.

But how do we reciprocate, how do we respond in love to the love of God? We respond by receiving that love given and walk in obedience thereafter. The greatest insult is to reject a gift given in love or to receive the gift and not walk in love; love is the trademark of follower of Jesus Christ (John 13:35). The second insult is not to walk in obedience because it disregards the value of the gift. Jesus said, "If you love me, you will obey my commands" (John 14:15).

Does God want us to love Him in return for the great love He showers upon us in creation and redemption? Yes! How? You shall love the Lord thy God with all your heart, with all your soul, with all your mind, and with all your strength (Mark 12:28-31). But it does not end there. God wants us to practice loving Him and loving our fellow human beings, because we are all created in God's image and likeness, and we are redeemed by the sacrifice of His Son (John 3:16).

But know this, God's love does not overrule His holiness; that is one reason obedience is necessary. To say God is all love, so I can defy the authority of His word and live anyway, is to misunderstand the holiness of God and the love of God. A person cannot live in his or her sins on the premise that God loves me and will not punish me. My love response calls for obedience. God hates sin! The sinner must repent, confess, and forsake his sin, receive the forgiveness of God, and walk in holiness and obedience. The penalty for sin is death, but the gift of God is eternal life through Jesus Christ our Lord (Romans 6:23). We practice holiness, not sin (1John 3:4-10).

The Attribute of Righteousness

Righteousness is another moral attribute of God; it is essential to His nature. Righteousness refers to "purity of heart and rectitude of life, being, and doing right." It is an attribute of God that is closely related to His holiness. It is "legislative or rectoral" because He is the righteous governor and judge over all his creatures (Unger 1988, 1081).[1] It is in God that "we live and move and have our being" (Acta 17:28).

When righteousness is used in reference to humans, it is speaking of right disposition which results in right doings or right behavior. Righteousness is inherently connected to the moral law of God. In other words, humans would not know what theft, adultery, idolatry, and murder are if there were no divine, moral laws prohibiting them. The moral law of God is written upon the heart of every human; that does not mean we are all restrained and guided by it perfectly.

THE GOD KIND OF LIFE - PART 1

God's moral law among humans goes back to the paradise garden, where God's law and human behavior first collided and resulted in death. This collision continued outside the garden, resulting in murder and death. Like his parents, Cain was punished for his violation of God's moral law. Fast forward, Moses did not invent the moral laws of God; he merely codified them.

God's righteousness desires of humans, more than right doing or right behavior, it demands a change in our nature within. For that reason, no person on his or her own can live up to God's required standard of righteousness. All humans have a sin nature that holds them into spiritual bondage and renders them incapable and powerless to conform to God's standard of righteousness satisfactorily (Roman 8:3-8).

Second Corinthians 5:21 tells that "Jesus Christ is the righteousness of God," which means He is God's acceptable standard. Jesus is the only human being that was able to meet God's standard of righteousness. Since we fall short of the glory of God, Jesus credits us with His righteous in the sense that He serves as our covering before God. Bible scholars and theologians refers to this as "imputed righteousness."

God provides our righteous covering in the person of Jesus Christ (Colossians 3:1-10). The prototype of this is seen immediately after the Fall of man, God provided the skin of an animal whose life He took to atone and cover His rebellious children (Genesis 3:21). Jesus the Lamb of God atones for our

A WORKING VACATION IN HEAVEN?

sins by His death on the cross to provide us the righteousness that covers us before the holy God (John 3:14-18).

When we are born again into the kingdom of God and adopted into His family, the righteousness of Jesus Christ is credited to our account (Romans 5:1-11). Jesus reigns in righteousness now, not only from heaven but in the life of each believer (Romans 6:22-23). And those lives He reigns in now are the ones that are qualified to reign with Him when His kingdom literally comes to earth (Matthew 6:9-11).

When Jesus returns, He will rule over the earth in "righteousness" from Jerusalem, sitting on the throne of David (Isaiah 9:6-7). This will be followed by His eternal reign with the Father from the New Jerusalem. In both His millennial and eternal reign, the people of God will reign with Him in righteousness (Revelation 21-22). This is what eternal life is all about; it is what we have in our gaze. It is what we are practicing for now, an eternal reign in righteousness with Jesus Christ and our heavenly Father.

What is required of us now is to repent of our sins and embrace Jesus Christ as our Savior and Lord. Once we have done that we must walk in faith, holiness, love and obedience. His grace is sufficient to keep us from falling (Jude 24).

In the next chapter, we will consider the other three moral attributes of God. When we truly know who God is, we come to know ourselves much better.

CHAPTER 7

THE GOD KIND OF LIFE
Part 2

The God kind of life is when human life reflects the character of God. The character of God is reflected in the moral attributes of God and in Jesus Christ. In the previous chapter we selected six of God's moral qualities to make the case; three are dealt with in that chapter. The other three are dealt with in this chapter, which are truth, Justice and mercy.

The Attribute of Truth

The first two institutions on earth are the family and human government, both presupposed the third, which is the nation.

A WORKING VACATION IN HEAVEN?

These institutions find their origin in God. It is God who started the family in the Paradise Garden. The mandate given to the man and the woman was to fill the earth with your kind; that implies nations (Genesis 2:26-28). A nation is a large family or a collective of many families as we see with the nation of Israel build upon the twelve sons of one man, Jacob.

When God, after the great Flood, protected the sanctity of life by enacting capital punishment, He instituted human government to enforce His law. The law He enacted then was this: "Whoever sheds human blood, by humans shall his blood be shed; for in the image of God has God made mankind" (Genesis 9:6). This law refers to murder such as Cain did to his brother earlier (Genesis 4:1-15). In the preamble to the law given to Noah, God said: "And for your lifeblood I will surely demand an accounting. I will demand an accounting from every animal. And from each human being, too, I will demand an accounting for the life of another human being" (Gen.9:5).

By virtue of giving humans' power to take human life in the case of murder, God instituted human government and put in their hand the sword of justice. We will return to this later.

Truth is the cement that holds a family or nation together. Without truth a family, nation, or society cannot develop trust; it will descend into chaos and confusion. The 2016 election in the United States with Donald J. Trump, is a vivid example of how a nation can fall into chaos when truth is dethroned and lies are exalted to take its place. Greater chaos awaits the nation should Trump get reelected in 2024.

The confusion that lies produce leads to anarchy, such as the insurrection on the seat of government in Washington, D.C., on January 6th, 2021. God who is the architect of the family and the nation knew that truth is essential for these institutions and society to function effectively.

But what is truth? Some say truth is subjective to person, time, and place. What they are saying is that your truth is not my truth, and what is true at one time may not be true at another time. And what is true in one place may not be true in another. Others say for a thing to be true it must either be factual, verifiable, honest, or faithful.

In general, we all agree that these elements are necessary in the determination of truthfulness. Christians embrace these elements as well, but they do not exactly constitute the Christian's definition of truth. To the authentic Christian, truth is objective and transcendent, personified, universal, and eternal. Let's unpack each term briefly.

First, truth is objective and transcendent. Truth is not something each person develops of himself or herself, and therefore, different from person to person, so your truth is not my truth. Truth is transcendent because it is a standard rooted in God's moral law, given to humans at creation, and later codified by Moses at God's command at Mount Sinai.

Second, to Christians, truth is personified. In this we also see objectivity. The embodiment of God's truth is Jesus Christ. Jesus said, "I am the way, the truth, and the life (John 14:6). Jesus is the truth; He is God's standard and model for human life. He is the perfect embodiment of God's moral law. What the written law could not do, Jesus did for us (Romans 8:3-4). Jesus is the personified, incarnate Word of God.

Third, to the Christian, truth is universal. It is the same everywhere. For this reason, authentic Christians are held to the same standard all over the world. Yes, certain cults and heretics do claim to be Christians, but they throw the word of God into the trash bin, therefore, they are not authentic.

Fourth, to the Chrisian truth is eternal. The eternality of truth is inherent in its transcendence and personification. Truth is rooted in God; it is part of His moral nature and essence. Whatever God does is true. His incarnate Word is true and eternal and His written word is true (John 1:1-5, 17:17).

The kingdom of God is not only the kingdom of light, but also the kingdom of truth. Everything that is contrary to God's truth is a lie, and the devil a liar. Jesus, the truth says, Satan is a liar and the father of all lies (John 8:44). God will rid His creation of all lies and liars (Revelation 20:10, 21:8).

The Attribute of Justice

Justice is part of God nature and therefore one of His moral attributes. It is important to note that where there is no justice there can be no righteousness, holiness, truth or peace. These attributes are interconnected; you cannot have one without the other. God is big on justice. Injustice gets God's attention speedily. Injustice is almost always the powerful taking advantage of the weak, the powerless, the voiceless. People put themselves on a collision course with God when they choose to act unjustly toward the powerless.

Because God is just, He wants to see justice in human relationships, fairness in our dealings with each other. God will overthrow wicked, oppressive rulers, and governments and bring judgment upon cruel nations. The liberation of the Israelites under Moses' leadership is one prime example of God's relentless justice at work to dismantle an oppressive regime, namely, Pharoh's government.

The Hebrew Bible is largely about justice. The first four of the Ten Commandments define human relationship with God. The other six define our relationship with our neighbors. They tell us that our neighbor's property is sacred. His wife, his donkey, his life are sacred. Therefore, don't covet your neighbor's wife, nor steal his property, lie to him, or murder him for God will avenge all such speedily.

It is God who defines the relationship between parents and children, wife and husband, master and servant, employer and employee (Exodus 20:12; Ephesians 5:22-25, 6:1-9).

God also made provision in the Law to protect the vulnerable of society: the poor, the widow, the fatherless. The prophet Micah trumpets God's demands of justice to the nation: "He has shown you, O man, what is good. And what does the Lord require of you? To do justly and to love mercy and to walk humbly with your God" (Micah 6:8).

Other than sin, the root cause of societal conflicts and conflicts between nations is injustice. The best of human leaders are selfish, they look mostly to their own interests, not the interest of others. King Solomon asserts that even in the hall of justice there is corruption. Because of human error, bribery, nepotism, and politics, some people never had justice. For these reasons, among others, there will be a *Final Judgment*, when the Just Judge will sit on the bench to render final justice to all (Revelation 20: 10-15).[1]

But before the Final Judgment, there will be the demonstration of a righteous and just society with a leader who rules in perfect righteousness and justice. That leader will be Jesus Christ Himself, God's model of righteous leadership. He will sit on the throne of David and rule in righteous and justice over the nations. This time is called, the *Millennium* (see Vol.7 in the series, "Related Events to the Second Coming of the Christ" by this author). The prophet Isaiah speaks of Christ's leadership in the *Millennium* as follows:

> For unto us a child is born. To us a son is given, and the government will be on his shoulders. And he will be called Wonderful Counselor, Mighty God, Everlasting Father, Prince of Peace. Of the greatness of his government and peace there will be no end. He will reign on David's throne and over his kingdom, establishing and upholding it with justice and righteousness from that time on and forever. The zeal of the LORD Almighty will accomplish this. (Isaiah 9:6-7)

THE GOD KIND OF LIFE - PART 2

The Millennium is followed by *The Final Judgment* (see Vol. 9 in the series). Then comes *The New World Order* (see Vol.10 in the series).

The New World Order of leadership is under God and Christ and the people of God—ruling over the new heaven and the new.[2] The New Jerusalen will beg the capital city and the seat of God's government (Revelation 21-22). It is a new world of eternal peace, righteousness, justice, and perfect prosperity. To be part of this City of God, you must register now that your name can be in the book of life.[3] How? By repenting of your sin, receive Jesus Christ as your Savior and Lord, and begin to the live the God kind of life, now!

The Attribute of Mercy

God is by nature merciful; mercy is another of His moral attributes. Mercy is the flip side of justice; it is like one coin with heads and tails. It is also connected to the love of God, the kindness of God, and the compassion of God.

God is infinitely perfect and all-powerful; we mortals are finite and imperfect. Therefore, in the administration of justice, God restrains Himself by mercy. This is beautifully expressed in the classic poem by Henry Francise Lyte, set to music by John Gross, "Father-like He tends and spares us; well, our feeble frame He knows; in His hand He gently bears us, rescues us from all our foes." God chastises his children, but in love (Hebrews 12). He does not abuse us.

A WORKING VACATION IN HEAVEN?

God wants the exercise of mercy in individual human relationships. The Micah 6:8 passage is applicable here as well; God wants us to "love mercy." In the Sermon on the Mount Jesus said, "Blessed are the merciful, for they shall obtain mercy" (Matthew 5:7 KJV). Mercy invites us to put ourselves in the other person's place and ask, how would like to be treated? When it is in your power to show mercy, do it! If you want to be forgiven, be willing to forgive those who trespass against you (Matthew 6:12-15).

Since, God instituted human government and gave them the power of the sword to execute judgment and justice, He has made it clear that human justice must be administered with mercy (Micah 6:8; Romans 13:1-7). For this reason of mercy, God gave His one and only Son as the Lamb of God for the redemption of the human family. We are all guilty of the violation of divine law and are under the sentence of death. But God in His mercy provides away out from the full arm of divine justice. He provides the basis for how we may be forgiven and receive the gift of eternal life (John 3:16).

Because of His mercy, God is patient or longsuffering toward us, giving us time to repent and accept His forgiveness, salvation, and gift on eternal life. If after all that we say no to God, we are saying we will pay our own way. This is where the word "not perish" in John 3:16 change to "will perish." We reject mercy and opt for full justice which is carried out here (Revelation 20:11-15). Showing mercy now is one way to express the God kind of life.

THE GOD KIND OF LIFE - PART 2

Conclusion

In chapters 6 and 7 we looked at the God kind of life that qualifies you and me to reign with Jesus Christ over the earth during the Millennium and to later over the new heaven, the new earth, and the New Jerusalem, eternally.

We begin to live and practice the God kind of life now; we enter it through a new birth experience in Jesus Christ (John 3:5-16). It is now, while we live in our physical body that we are given entrance to the kingdom of God and adopted into the family of God. The gift of eternal life must be received now to qualify to reign with Jesus Christ later (John 3:16).

In these two chapters we cover six of the moral attributes of God: holiness, love, righteousness, truth, justice, and mercy. These qualities must be reflected in our lives, and it is not difficult because it is not in our own strength, we do it.

When we are born again, the Holy Spirit takes up residence in us, and by yielding control to Him we are able to live out these six and more attributes of God. The apostle Paul gives us an example of nine graces cultivated by the blessed Holy Spirit in our lives (Galatians 6:22-23).

The attribute of holiness reminds us we are called to live a separated life, a sanctified life. It demands repentance and a turning away from our sins. We are saved from our sins, not in our sins (Matthew 1:21). You cannot be a practicing adultery, thief, liar, homosexual, drunkard and inherit eternal life; we must turn away from these practices (1 Corinthians 6:9-11; Revelation 22:14-15).

A WORKING VACATION IN HEAVEN?

The attribute of love teaches us that God is love, but this love is not permissive; it makes demands and us, it disciplines us (Hebrews 12:5-13). The true evidence that we love God is the practice of obedience to His word (John 13:34-35, 14:13).

The attribute of righteousness guides us in the correct manner of life. We are not able to produce this quality of righteousness on our own; it is imputed to us by Jesus Christ. We receive it when we truly repent and put on Christ who is our righteousness (Romans 5:1-7, 8:3-4).

The attribute of truth reminds us that God is truth, the Holy Spirit is the Spirit of truth, and Jesus is truth personified. God's truth is universal, and eternal.

The attribute of justice reveals that God is just and will hold all of us accountable for the life we lead in the body. Because He is just, he wants justice in human relationships. For this same reason of being just, there will be a Final Judgment to render final justice (Revelation 20:11-15).

The attribute of mercy teaches that God by nature is merciful to all His creatures. For that reason, He restrains His great power by mercy. He wants humans to show mercy toward each other and in their administration of justice (Micah 6:8). These attributes are examples of the God kind of life God demands of us now to qualify to reign with Him later. They are made possible through a born-again relationship with Jesus Christ (John 3:16).

REFERENCES

Chapter 1

1. Butterfield, *Rosaria. Five Lies of Our Anti-Christian Age.* Wheaton, Illinois: Crossway Publishers, 2023.

2. Dewar, Michael W. *The Rapture. Vol.1.* Brooklyn, NY: Dwelling Place Publishers, 2022.

Chapter 2

1. Dewar, Michael W. *The Second Coming of the Christ.* Vol.5. Brooklyn, NY: Dwelling Place Publishers, 2023.

2. _____. *The Great Tribulation Survival Guide…*, Vol.3. Brooklyn, NY: Dwelling Place Publishers, 2021.

3. _____. *The Believers Judgment and Rewards.* Vol.2. Brooklyn, NY: Dwelling Place Publishers, 2022.

4. _____. *The Believers Judgment and Rewards.*

5. Unger, Merrill F. R.K. Harrison, Editor. *The New Unger's Bible Dictionary*. Chicago IL: Moody Bible Institute, 1988.

Chapter 3

1. Dewar, Michael W. *The Millennium: A Thousand Years of Peace and Prosperity.* Vol.7. Brooklyn, NY: Dwelling Place Publishers, 2023.
2. _____. *The New World Order. Vol.10.* Brooklyn NY: Dwelling Place Publishers, 2023.

Chapter 4

1. "Entropy" at https://en.wikipedia.org/wiki/Entropy.

2. Dewar, Michael W. *Resurrection of Humans.*Vol.8. Brooklyn, NY: Dwelling Place Publishers, 2023.

Chapter 5

1. Dewar, Michael W. *The Final Judgment.*Vol.9. Brooklyn, NY: Dwelling Place Publishers, 2023.

2. _____. *The New World Order*. Vol.10. Brooklyn, NY: Dwelling Place Publishers, 2023.

3. https://einstein.stanford.edu/SPACETIME/spacetime2.html
4. https://www.pbs.org/wgbh/nova/article/how-many-dimensions-does-the-universe-really-have/
5. Ibid.

REFERENCES

6. Ibid.
7. **Dewar, Michael W.** *The Coronation of the Christ & the Marriage Supper.* Vol.4. Brooklyn, NY: Dwelling Place Publishers, 2023.

Chapter 6

1. Unger, Merrill F. The New Unger's Bible Dictionary. Chicago, IL: Moody Bible Institute, 1988.

Chapter 7

1. Dewar, Michael W. The Final Judgment

2. _____. The New World Order. Vol.10.

3. _____. *The Book of Life & The Books of Wrath.* Brooklyn, NY: Dwelling Place Publishers, 2023.

A WORKING VACATION IN HEAVEN?

OTHER BOOKS BY THIS AUTHOR

Series: Related Events to the Second Coming of the Christ (10 volumes):

Vol. 1   Vol. 2

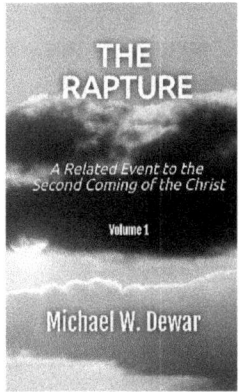 

A WORKING VACATION IN HEAVEN?

Vol.3

Vol. 4

Vol.5

Vol.6

OTHER BOOKS BY THIS AUTHOR

Vol.7 **Vol.8**

Vol.9 **Vol.10**

A WORKING VACATION IN HEAVEN?

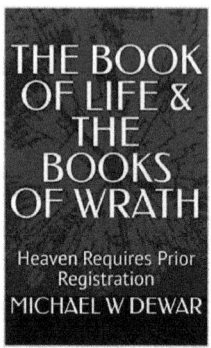
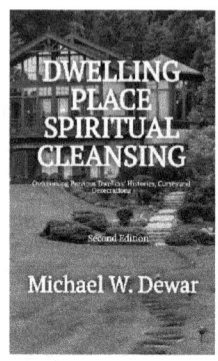

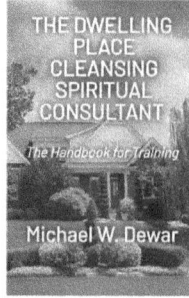

The consultant book is a course of study for those who wish to become certified to conduct "Dwelling Place Spiritual Cleansing." The other book of similar title is the textbook. Everybody needs to read the main text; you can do your own spiritual cleansing.

OTHER BOOKS BY THIS AUTHOR

This book is also the textbook for launching a peace ministry at your church. It comes with an Instructor's Manual and Students' Manual, both sold separately. Used for individual and group study.

Instructor's Manual   **Students' Manual**

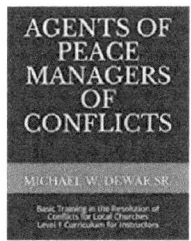 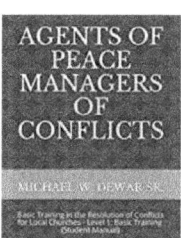

Students will need the textbook and students' manual.

A WORKING VACATION IN HEAVEN?

CONTACT US

Join our email list as well.

DPSCleansing.com or DeDwelling.com

Email us at: CS@DPSCleansing.com

ABOUT THE AUTHOR

Michael W. Dewar, Sr. is a pastor, Bible teacher, and mentor in the spiritual life for more than forty years. He is also a specialist in conflict management and resolution. He authors a three-volume course of study in church conflicts, and how to launch a peace ministry in the local church.

He holds advanced degrees from several institutions of higher learning, including the Master of Divinity, the Master of Social Work, and an earned doctorate.

Reverend Dewar is the founder and pastor of the New York Congregational Baptist Church (NYCBC). He lives in New York with his family. He is the author of the 10-volume series, "Related Events to the Second Coming of the Christ."

A WORKING VACATION IN HEAVEN?

www.ingramcontent.com/pod-product-compliance
Lightning Source LLC
Chambersburg PA
CBHW071717040426
42446CB00011B/2107